PRAISE FOR BOOKS BY RUTH BEH

An Island Called Home: Returning to Jewi
Photographs by Humberto Mayol

"A fascinating and vital memoir about a rarely glimpsed cultural force in Cuba.... *An Island Called Home* digs deep to reveal new things about the collective soul of the Cubans." —**Oscar Hijuelos**, author of *The Mambo Kings Play Songs of Love*

"*An Island Called Home* is a kaddish, an offering, dedicated to the exiles and to the children of the exiles and for those wandering still, searching for their homes. May they 'not be given up for lost.'"
—**Sandra Cisneros**, author of *Caramelo*

"Ruth Behar's personal account of the last Jews of Cuba moved me to tears. Courageous, keenly observed, and beautifully written, *An Island Called Home* is cultural anthropology that rises to the level of great literature. A masterpiece!" —**Aaron Lansky**, founder and president, the National Yiddish Book Center

"*An Island Called Home* is Ruth Behar at her best. Her caring for Cuba and its small and thought-provoking Jewish life is profound."
—**Virginia Dominguez**, author of *People as Subject, People as Object: Selfhood and Peoplehood in Contemporary Israel*

"*An Island Called Home* weaves past and present with poetic strength. The searing images here made brilliant by words and photographs connect the personal with the communal." —**Hasia Diner**, Paul and Sylvia Steinberg Professor of American Jewish History, New York University

"This may be Behar's most personal work.... She lovingly intertwines her own thoughts and feelings with the more analytical observations of her profession. The result: a narrative that tugs at the heart."
—**Ana Veciana-Suarez**, *The Miami Herald*

"Behar preserves in memory the people and places that make up Cuba's Jewish story." —*Publishers Weekly*

"Behar takes her readers on a journey that provokes, inspires, moves, and satisfies. There are few ethnographies that are at once so intellectually rich and aesthetically fulfilling, so accessible and so stimulating."
—**Shari Jacobson,** *American Ethnologist*

"To capture and share such intimate stories while preserving their tellers' dignity requires artistry. Behar has it, and her readers are the luckier for that."
—**Joel Streicker,** *Forward.com*

"Anyone with an interest in what is left of the Jewish communities of the world will be grateful for Behar and Mayol's contemporary snapshots of Cuban Jewish life." —**Carol Cook,** *Haaretz*

The Vulnerable Observer: Anthropology That Breaks Your Heart

"Behar . . . describes herself as 'a woman of the border: between places, between identities, between languages, between cultures, between longings and illusions, one foot in the academy and one foot out.' It is a forceful mix that infuses her vision with insight, candor, and compassion."
—**Diane Cole,** *The New York Times Book Review*

"A story that engages the emotions. Making the past visible, [Behar] preserves it against oblivion." —**Stanley Trachtenberg,** *The Washington Post Book World*

"Behar has convinced me that ethnographic empathy will produce an anthropology that has greater meaning than the distanced and detached academic anthropology of the past." —**Barbara Fisher,** *The Boston Globe*

"Her luminous essays build cultural bridges and challenge conventional ways of doing anthropology." —*Publishers Weekly*

"Beautifully crafted, thoughtful, evocative, and full of unexpected juxtapositions that bring ever deepening insights." —**Marjorie L. DeVault,** *Contemporary Sociology*

"Memories do not vanish; they recede and leave traces. The anthropologist who makes herself vulnerable to these indications makes the world a more intelligible and hopeful place." —**Judith Bolton-Fasman,** *The Jerusalem Report*

Bridges to Cuba/Puentes a Cuba

"A finely crafted, readable cross-cultural encounter between *dos comadres*: feminist anthropologist and informant, *cubanita de este lado* and *mexicana* across the border. . . . *Escribiendo cultura con corazón, compasión y pasión*, Behar moves the serpent to speak, and moves us to read and read again."
—**Gloria Anzaldúa**, author of *Borderlands/La Frontera*

"Ruth Behar, as editor of *Bridges to Cuba/Puentes a Cuba*, leaps across conventional intellectual boundaries in an effort to show the complexity of nationhood, exile, and revolution in the Cuban experience of the last thirty years. An important book about the possibility and impossibility of building cultural and political bridges."
—**Arcadio Díaz-Quiñones**, Professor Emeritus, Princeton University

"*Bridges to Cuba* is the first U.S. anthology that looks at Cuban creativity from an integrated perspective, refusing to kneel before the painful and often arbitrary divisions that have split the voices of this passionate culture into forever separate bands. The results are magnificent."
—**Margaret Randall**, author of *Women in Cuba: Twenty Years Later*

"*Bridges to Cuba* is essential reading for Cuba-watchers who want to go beyond traditional social science research to appreciate the extraordinary cultural talent of Cubans." —**John M. Kirk and Peter McKenna**, *Latin American Research Review*

Translated Woman: Crossing the Border with Esperanza's Story

"Esperanza's story is a stunning critique and reversal of the received image of the passive and humble Mexican Indian woman. . . . Behar has broken many taboos and inhibitions in writing an experimental ethnographic text that has for its subject a poor native Mexican woman who refuses to be a pitiful victim, or a saint, or a Madonna, or a whore, or a Joan of Arc."
—**Nancy Scheper-Hughes**, *The New York Times Book Review*

"Part anthropological study, part gripping oral history, part personal confession, and part feminist cry of outrage, *Translated Woman* is a brave and unusual work." —**Pamela Constable**, *The Boston Globe*

"A tour de force." —**Judith Friedlander**, *American Ethnologist*

"A demanding and intensely satisfying read." —**Beverly Sanchez,** *Hispanic Magazine*

"A landmark in contemporary anthropology. . . . An important effort in the direction of more thoughtful and inclusive ways of knowing." —**Gelya Frank,** *American Anthropologist*

PRAISE FOR *TRAVELING HEAVY: A MEMOIR IN BETWEEN JOURNEYS*

"*Traveling Heavy* . . . is the product of a poetic mind, and the work itself can be regarded as prose poetry. . . . Behar has not recovered from her 'interrupted childhood' in Havana, and it is this tragedy that makes her who she is, that shapes the ghosts she pursues, that has guided her steps as a subjective anthropologist; and that is able to offer the reader a smörgåsbord of literary delights."
—**Marion Fischel**, *The Jerusalem Post*

"A heartfelt witness to the changing political and emotional landscape of the Cuban-American experience." —*Kirkus Reviews*

"[As] the offspring of the union of Ashkenazi and Sephardic Jewish families. . . . [Behar's] displacement within her own people forges a unique empathy for the communities that she studies and their stories that she records."
—**Judy Bolton-Fasman**, *The Boston Globe*

"Ruth Behar displays her Kafkaesque dislocation. She descends from a long line of travelers by necessity, exiled from their homelands for reasons both political and social. . . . Through the act of composing a memoir about her search, she writes the lost homeland and the lost self into existence." —**Jane Shmidt**, *Bookslut*

"I hungrily absorbed the experiences of [Behar's] continued quest . . . drawn in equally by her alluring tales and storytelling style."
—**Miriam Bradman Abrahams**, *Jewish Book Council*

"[Behar's] story is one that, while singular, carries a universal resonance at a time when immigration is often in the news and America continues to wrestle with a growing Latino population. Not only is her story of trying to let go of physical and emotional baggage a significant one, but the sense of reclamation of identity, of returning home or even figuring out home is par*ticularly timely*."
—**Joshunda Sanders**, *Kirkus Feature*

"All those intrigued by their ancestral story will be moved by [Behar's] personal quest and also by how—with the help of computers as well as the kindness of strangers—the lost can find their way home."
—**Hazel Rochman**, *Booklist Online*

"A moving story of finding oneself through a lifetime of travel."
—**Olga Wise**, *Library Journal*

"*Traveling Heavy* is a collection of pieces that weave together a story well worth reading for years to come." —**Jacquelyn Lazo**, *ForeWord Reviews*

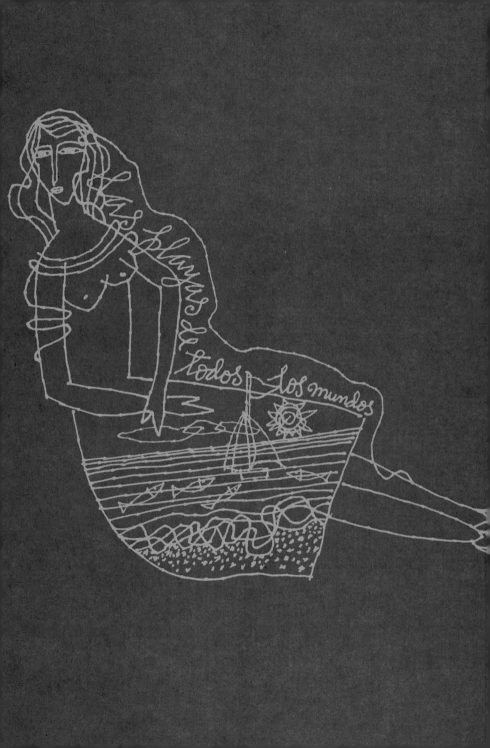

TRAVELING HEAVY

a memoir in between journeys

Ruth Behar

Duke University Press *Durham and London* 2013

Designed by Amy Ruth Buchanan
Typeset in Garamond Premier Pro
by Copperline Book Services, Inc.

Frontispiece: Rolando Estévez,
original drawing from the handmade
book, Bertha Caluff Pagés, *Las playas
de todos los mundos (El Alfa el
Omega)*, Ediciones Vigía, Matanzas,
Cuba, 2007.

*The author and Duke University Press
gratefully acknowledge the University
of Michigan, Office of the Vice
President for Research and the College
of Literature, Science, and the Arts,
which provided funds toward the
publication of this book.*

ISBN 978-0-8223-5720-9 (pbk :
alk. paper)

The Library of Congress has cataloged
the hardcover edition as follows:
Behar, Ruth
Traveling heavy : a memoir in
between journeys / Ruth Behar.
p. cm.
ISBN 978-0-8223-5467-3 (cloth :
alk. paper)
1. Behar, Ruth 2. Jews, Cuban—
United States—Biography.
3. Cuban Americans—Biography.
4. Jews—Cuba—Biography. I. Title.
F1789.J4B43 2013
305.892'4073092—dc23
2012044741

TO MY FAMILY
and the strangers who have
treated me like family

CONTENTS

ILLUSTRATIONS

Let no thought pass incognito, and keep
your notebook as strictly as the authorities
keep their register of aliens.
—WALTER BENJAMIN,
"One-Way Street," *Reflections* (1928)

part one

FAMILY

Immigrants just arrived in New York.
Left to right: Papi, Ruth, Mami, and Mori,
1962. Photographer unknown.

the key to the house

....

I love to travel.

But I'm also terrified of traveling.

As I embark on yet another trip, I carefully enact my various good luck rituals. I check to be sure that my Turkish evil eye bracelet is still around my wrist. If there's turbulence during the flight, I'll rub the turquoise glass beads to keep the plane from falling out of the sky. In a zippered pouch inside my purse, I place a handmade necklace I must have with me at all times to be protected from illness and sudden death. I received it at a Santería ceremony in Cuba, where the hypnotic beat of three batá drums summoned the ancient African deities back to earth. Carrying these talismans, one evocative of my Jewish heritage and the other of my Cuban heritage, I ready myself for travel.

Before I go out the door, I drop my car and office keys on a side table, since they won't be of any use while I'm away. But I say to myself, "Take the key to the house. Don't go anywhere without that key."

The legend is that Sephardic Jews took the keys to their houses when they were expelled from Spain over five hundred years ago. Centuries later, living in other lands, they still had those keys in their possession. Tucking my house key in my suitcase, I honor the sad love for Spain that my exiled ancestors clung to.

Of course I know perfectly well that my stay-at-home husband, David, will open the door on my return. (In fact, he always drops me off and picks me up at the airport.) When we were young, David and I went everywhere together, but now that we're older I'm the one who travels. He stays behind in Michigan, *cuidando la casa*, as they like to say in Mexico, minding the house. Even with the assurance that David awaits me on my return, I fear that if I don't bring my key a catastrophe will happen that will prevent me from coming home.

I may rack up miles flying far and wide, but travel isn't something I can treat casually. My departures are always filled with a looming sense of finality. Minutes before take-off, Mami calls, wishing me well in such a choked voice it seems she's uttering a last goodbye. "Please call me when you land, Ruti, don't forget," she says. By the time we hang up, I'm trembling. Then I turn around and call my son, Gabriel, in New York and make him totally nervous. "Bye, honey. Love you, honey," I say, as if I won't ever see him again.

Then it's time to power off. There's nothing left to do but hold my breath as the flight attendant shuts the door of the plane. I'm immediately overcome by a sense of tender solidarity, bringing me to the edge of tears, as I glance at my fellow travelers: the businessman who helped me squeeze my bulging suitcase into the overhead bin, the tired mother clutching her crying baby, the tattooed young man clasping his headphones, waiting to be up in the air so he can listen to his music, the lovers holding hands like schoolchildren, all of us united in the belief that it's not our day to die.

Yes, I'm a pretty neurotic nomad.

What's funny is that in spite of traveling heavy with my doubts and worries, just give me the flimsiest pretext to get on a plane and go somewhere, and I'll rush to pack my suitcase. Not that packing is easy for me. Faced with the quandary of what to bring and what to leave, I suffer deciding what's got to stay behind. Is it too melodramatic to say that packing is a rehearsal for death, when you can't take anything with you? Traveling, you can take only a couple of things, and this gets you used to letting go of the material world. It sweetens the coming of the inevitable departure. You abandon the weightiness of your existence so you can be light on your feet as you move about in a new place, meet new people.

I go to other places for the same reasons most everyone does: to seek out a change of scenery and feel a sense of enchantment, to learn about the lives of strangers, and to give myself a chance to be someone I can't be at home. We leave behind the creature comforts and familiarity of home in order to explore alternate worlds, alternate selves.

Travelers are those who go elsewhere because they want to, because they can afford to displace themselves. Immigrants are those who go elsewhere because they have to. If they don't displace themselves they'll suffer: their very existence is at risk. They pick up and leave, sometimes at a moment's notice. The journey is wrenching, often dangerous, a loss of the known world, a change of scenery that creates estrangement, an uneasy dwelling among strangers, having to become a different person against one's will.

I'm now a traveler, a professional traveler. Until I went to college, I had no idea there was a profession called cultural anthropology, in which it's *my job* to spend extended periods of time residing elsewhere, doing fieldwork to understand how people in other places find meaning in their lives. From the first moment, I was seduced by the prospect of being such a traveler. And so I set off on this odd career, and everywhere I went I found a semblance of home. The kindness of strangers was a great gift. I would not be who I am without it.

So now I'm a traveler, but I always remember I started out in life being an immigrant. We left Cuba when I was four and a half and my brother, Mori, was just a toddler. There's an old black-and-white picture of the two of us, with Mami and Papi, taken upon our arrival in

New York. We're wearing our best travel clothes and squinting into the sun and our future. We look bedraggled, shabby, a little shy, and grateful. Our posture is lopsided. We're unsure of ourselves.

Caro, the woman who was my nanny long ago in Cuba, says I was happily oblivious when we left the island. "You thought you were going on a holiday, you didn't realize you were leaving," she tells me. Perhaps a child is incapable of mourning the loss of a homeland. I've been accused sometimes (though *never* by fellow Cubans) of having left too young to assert my right to claim a bond to Cuba. What I know for sure is that I found it painfully difficult to adjust to life in the United States. To this day, no matter where I go, I carry the memory of the girl who felt utterly foreign, helpless, speechless, a misfit, the girl who wanted to dissolve into the cracks in the walls.

I don't recall the moment in my childhood when I was uprooted, taken from the place where I belonged. My subconscious gave me amnesia so I'd have to keep traveling to find the girl who lost her home and didn't cry because she didn't know what she was losing.

Call me an anthropologist who specializes in homesickness. Going to other places is how I make my living. I'm forever packing and unpacking a suitcase. I should know how to travel light. But I travel heavy. I carry too much.

Among anthropologists it's a mortal sin to write about oneself. We're taught to be scribes, to tell other people's stories. Here I've gone and written personally, too personally. But being an obedient student at heart, I've done so with trepidation. This is the memoir I snuck in, between journeys.

learning english with shotaro

....

I have spoken English for almost fifty years and still haven't forgotten that English isn't my first language. Even now I hesitate as I lay down this first sentence. Does it sound right in English? Is it stilted? Is it correct to say "I have" and "haven't" and "isn't" in the same sentence? I honestly don't—do not—know.

It's strange and possibly absurd that I should feel this way. I speak English perfectly well. I wrote my Ph.D. thesis in English. I think, dream, and live much of my life in the English language. "You're from Cuba?" people say, surprised. "But you don't have an accent." No, I don't have an accent. I don't say "shit" when I want to say "sheet," as my mother does, though as a teenager I tried hard to imitate a British accent because I considered it more refined than the English I heard around me as I was growing up in New York. I spoke to my parents only in Spanish, as I do even today, because Spanish is the language in which they're most comfortable.

Mami and Papi definitely have accents, thick Cuban accents, when they speak English, and I continue to correct their pronunciation and grammatical errors, as I did as a child. English was the public language, the language of power, competition, and progress—also the language of solitude, the language in which I was totally on my own, without my parents to help me. Now I speak an English that can't be recognized as being from anywhere specific. Years ago, my brother, Mori, put it

DEC • 63

Birthday party in Queens
Left to right: Dinah, Cora,
Shotaro, and, seated, cousin

exactly right. What I have, he told me, is a "college accent." It's the English of a person who went to school, studied hard, and got good grades because she feared if she didn't, she'd be sent back to the dumb class.

No one can tell by looking at me or hearing me speak that another language burns inside me, an invisible but unquenchable flame. No one can tell I came to the English language the way a woman in another era came to her husband in an arranged marriage, trying to make the best of a relationship someone else chose for her and hoping one day she'd fall in love. I'm still waiting. . . . I depend on English. I'm grateful I speak English. I wouldn't be a professor, a scholar, a traveler, a writer if I didn't know English. But I'm not in love with English.

My mother tongue is Spanish. This is the language I spoke as a little girl in Cuba. I'm told I spoke that little girl's Spanish with a lot of spunk. They tell me I was a nonstop talker, *una cotorrita* (a little parrot). But after we arrived in the United States, I grew shy, silent, sullen. I have no memory of myself as a little girl speaking Spanish in Cuba. That's likely why every time I'm in Cuba and encounter a little girl letting Spanish roll off her tongue so naturally, so effortlessly, I want to yell, "That was me!" That was me, once upon a time— before I became self-conscious about which *lengua*, which tongue, I was speaking.

When we left Cuba after the Revolution and went to Israel, I'm told I became fluent in Hebrew. I might have already known a few words because in Havana I attended kindergarten at the Centro Israelita, a bilingual Spanish-Yiddish day school founded by Jewish immigrants who settled in Cuba in the 1920s and 1930s. But Hebrew didn't stick in our family. Leaving Israel for New York after a year, we never spoke it at home. Hebrew became the language of the liturgy, of our infrequent prayers, on the High Holy Days and Passover; it ceased to be a vernacular tongue for us. Spanish became our home language, and I spoke it with Abuelo and Abuela, my Ladino-speaking grandparents from

Turkey, and also with Baba and Zayde, my Yiddish-speaking grandparents from Poland and Russia.

Just before I turned six, I was dropped into a first-grade classroom at P.S. 117 in Queens. I was expected to survive without being able to utter a word of English. This was in 1962, before bilingual programs and English as a Second Language were introduced into the public school system. You learned English by osmosis, ear training, lip reading, like a baby, without any special instruction and not a drop of mercy. Or you failed to learn English and joined the dumb class, where you stayed forever.

In that first-grade classroom, I vividly recall the teacher, Mrs. Sarota, writing a math problem on the blackboard. Knowing the answer, I raised my hand. Mrs. Sarota smiled and nodded, lifted her eyebrows. She waited, chalk in hand. I opened my mouth. No words came out. I knew the answer, but didn't know how to say it in English. I sat there. "Ruth," the teacher said, "do you know the answer or not?" I wasn't accustomed to hearing my name spoken in English. It sounded harsh. Ugly. In my family, I'm called Ruti, and the two syllables are said slowly, languorously.

"Well, Ruth?" The teacher spoke my name like an insult. I tried sign language, writing the answer in the air with my fingers. Soon the other children were giggling and pointing at me, as though I were a monkey escaped from the zoo. Ashamed, I lowered my head and pretended to disappear. I retreated into silence for the rest of the school year.

By second grade I was in the dumb class and felt I deserved to be there. Although the school claimed not to make any distinctions, as kids we knew that, for each grade, there was a dumb class made up of children who'd flunked the previous year. To be in the dumb class in second grade was a sure sign you'd gotten off to a lousy start in life. Things had to be pretty bad for a kid to flunk first grade. The teacher, whose name I've forgotten, acted as if we were not merely dumb but deaf as well; she repeated things and hovered over us, watching as we wrote in our notebooks, ready to pounce on our mistakes. Some of the kids in the class were slow learners, but a few were more impaired, like Grace, who had a large head and wore shoes several sizes too large and was so friendly you knew something had to be wrong with her. In those days, the dumb class was also where they put the foreign kids until they could prove to the world they were actually smart and had just needed to learn English—or until they revealed that deep down they really were dumb.

Shotaro, a boy from Japan, was also in the dumb class because he spoke a language that wasn't English. As the only two foreign kids, Shotaro and I became close friends. His bangs were crooked and he was a head shorter than I, so I felt protective of him. We looked at picture books together and read to each other and played tag and hopscotch during recess. Shotaro was the only boy from school I invited to my birthday party in second grade. (Mori and my cousin Danny were there too, but they didn't count.) He came outfitted like a little man, in a gray suit, white shirt, and maroon tie. I wore one of my old handmade Cuban dresses that barely fit me but which I still adored. Not long after, all the dresses from Cuba disappeared from my closet; my mother gave them to my cousin Linda. It pained me to see her wearing them.

One of the pictures I most recall from those years, which I've since lost, is the Polaroid of a cluster of girls around an M&M-studded cake, with Shotaro and me in the middle of the group, beaming from the sheer joy of standing next to each other (But I did find a picture in which I'm wearing a crown, Grace appears on my left, and Shotaro stands on the edge, sporting a party hat.) I think Shotaro and I learned to speak English only because of our urgent need to communicate with one another, though there existed an understanding between us, mysterious and deep, that went beyond words.

We both did well and got good at English. By the end of the school year we were sprung from the dumb class and assigned to a regular third-grade class. But Shotaro and I didn't continue together in third grade. His family decided to return to Japan, whereas it had become clear to my family that there wasn't going to be any return to Cuba.

I was sad to see Shotaro go. He gave me a going-away present that I still store at my parents' house with other keepsakes from my childhood. It is a pair of miniature wooden male and female dolls, outfitted in matching kimonos and nested together in a silk brocade box. Maybe the dolls were intended to represent the two of us, a girl and a boy, who grew into the English language together, during a year spent in the dumb class. Neither of us spoke the other's language, so English was our common tongue—English and a faith that we weren't dumb, that what we were was dispossessed, dislocated.

el beso

....

The first boy to put his tongue in my mouth was Puerto Rican. The tip of his tongue touched my tongue, then his entire tongue twirled around so forcefully I was afraid I'd choke. Stunned, I hardly had time to react. On the beach, in Miami, we nearly collapsed onto the sand from the effort, but he managed to catch me in his arms before we both fell. The sun was low in the sky. The ocean had fallen silent. His tongue tasted of smooth sand, mint, and blooming young manhood.

I was twelve; he was just two or three years older, but I thought of him as much, much older. And definitely more "experienced." Boys, I was being instructed by my mother, would always know more about such things than girls. As I helped Mami prepare dinner every night in our crowded kitchen in New York, our eyes tearing from the fried onions that went into the black beans and every other dish she cooked, she'd issue her stern warnings. Boys had to know more because they were boys. Developing into men, they'd need to have sex, *la cosa del hombre* required it, *no sé si entiendes, mi niña,* but they can't hold themselves back—if they don't have it, they'll go crazy, they'll explode, so don't tempt a man, because he can't stop himself. It's *la cosa,* their thing, their *cosa* is like that—it's not their fault, they have to have it, so say no. Say no. Remember, say no before things go too far. *Trata de entender, mi niña. No te dejes. Di que no.* Don't let them convince you. They don't have anything to lose. *La que pierde es siempre la mujer. No te*

olvides de eso. Wait. Wait until you find *un hombre bueno, un hombre que te quiera de verdad, un hombre* who doesn't want you just for that. *Ten cuidado,* okay? Be careful.

Counterposed to this message to fear sex and refrain from sex in order to save myself for the good man who'd love me enough to bridle his animal needs was my father's education of Mori, as early as the age of ten, in the ways of desire with laughter, humor, and brash joy. On lazy Sunday mornings after brunch, my father and Mori would lie together in bed in their pajamas, my father sharing with my little brother his stash of *Playboys,* whose hiding place inside the drawer of his night table I'd long since discovered. As my father gazed at the pictures with Mori, he seemed to say, For you this legacy, *mi niño.* Because you are a boy, for you a taste of all the delicious fruits of a woman's body. Soon they will be yours to squeeze and smell and savor and let drip from your lips like the sweetest, the juiciest of mangoes.

I don't remember how I met the Puerto Rican boy who gave me his tongue to taste. I know he was Puerto Rican from Spanish Harlem. I forgot his name, or maybe I never knew it. He was skinny and long-limbed with thick jet-black hair. I had no idea where he was staying or who he was with in Miami. All he knew about me was that I was Cuban and lived in Queens—in Forest Hills, not in the ritzy part, near the tennis courts and mansions, but close to 108th Street. At least there were trees that turned green in summer, and there was a lobby (though no doorman) in our building, the Carol Apartments, where we'd just moved. And he knew I was a chubby girl, desperately ill at ease in my red two-piece bathing suit edged with a sad blue ruffle, with eyes already cloudy from reading too many books, and pathetically innocent of the pleasure my body was made for. We'd meet on the beach, kiss, and ask no questions.

Our kissing took place in Miami Beach in July, when the sea grows warm as a steam bath. My parents and their friends in *El Grupo,* a group of Cuban Jews who formed close bonds during the early years of immigration to New York, had begun to make enough money by the late 1960s that they felt they could afford a vacation. Someone found out that during the summer—the low season—hotels on Collins Avenue slashed their prices in half since their better clients, the *americanos*, preferred to winter in the sun. One of the *El Grupo* dads, I think it was Ysrael, the engineer, whom everyone called the Senator because he was so smart, did the research and decided that the Surfcomber Hotel offered the best deal: two meals a day and two double beds, and the kids stayed free and had a lifeguard to watch them at the pool.

Off we'd go, five *El Grupo* couples and their children, to scorch our skin in the blazing summer sun, drink frosty hot pink *mamey* milkshakes, remember Cuba, and forget how grim and gray life was in New York. The *El Grupo* fathers would come for a hard-earned two weeks of vacation, then they'd depart, changing out of bathing suits and donning business suits to return to work in New York and keep earning enough so the *El Grupo* mothers could have two extra weeks in Miami Beach with the children.

How free and easy were those two weeks without the fathers—no scoldings, no demands, no tensions, no arguments. How happy they looked, Miriam, Zelmi, Fanny, Nina, and my mother, lounging around the pool, their bodies slick with suntan oil, their breasts pouring jubilantly out of their bathing suits, and no man to tell them, *Oye, estás ensenañando mucho,* their nails pearly with polish so that they looked like seashells, and without a care in the world, the ladies of leisure as they might've been in Cuba had the Revolution not disrupted their lives so rudely. And we *Grupo* children, how gloriously wild we were allowed to be during those fatherless two weeks, jumping into and out of the pool, no one admonishing us about how we were going to get paralyzed if we didn't wait long enough after eating to go swimming.

It was during one of those blessed weeks when the *Grupo* mothers were alone with us children that I began to learn how to kiss like a woman.

But my education was cut short.

One afternoon, just after a kissing session, I climbed back to the pool area from the beach and noticed Mami and Mori watching me with strange looks on their faces. I waved hello and tried to act nonchalant, but Mami wasted no time getting to the point. Where had I been? Why hadn't I told her I had a boyfriend?

What do you mean? What boyfriend? I asked, ineptly feigning ignorance.

Giggling at first, Mami said Mori had seen me with the boy, and he'd told her. She didn't believe him, so Mori said, "Okay, let's spy on Ruti," and the two of them had hidden and witnessed me kissing the boy, clear as day. As she was telling me this, my mother broke out in peals of laughter. Both she and Mori had laughed so hard watching me, she said, it was all they could do to muffle their laughter—that's how funny it was. Had I really not heard them?

I'd heard nothing. Now I'd heard too much. I glanced over at Mori. He had a sheepish grin and looked sorry that he'd gotten me into trouble. He'd just thought it hilarious to discover that his shy and bookish older sister was making out with a boy, and he hadn't been able to resist telling. I vowed never to trust my brother again.

Wiping away her laughter tears, Mami asked, "*¿Y quién es el muchacho?*" Who was this boy? I hardly knew. I hardly wanted to know.

"He's just a boy I met."

"*No parece* Jewish," she said.

I shrugged. "He's Puerto Rican."

"*¿Puertorriqueño? ¿Estás loca, Ruti?*"

Her face grew deadly serious, as if I'd just said the boy was from Mars or contaminated with a rare form of the bubonic plague that had survived the Middle Ages.

"Thank god your father isn't here," she said, putting her palm to her chest and sighing.

"And what's wrong with him being Puerto Rican? We're Cubans, aren't we?" I exclaimed, feeling very clever indeed.

"*Pero Ruti, tú que eres tan inteligente, tan* smart. *¿Tu no sabes* that we're Jewish? You're too young to be kissing any boys, *pero ¿cómo pudiste besar un puertorriqueño? Ay, Ruti, un puertorriqueño, ¡Por tu vida! Ruti, ¿tu no sabes cómo son los puertorriqueños?* They have dirty minds. *Solamente quieren una cosa.* They want only one thing from girls. *¿Cómo te dejaste, Ruti?* And you're so smart. *No lo puedo creer. Menos mal que tu padre no está aquí. Te mata si está aquí.* Please, don't ever see that boy again. If your father finds out, he'll kill me too for not stopping you."

Only later would I fully comprehend the depth and consequences of the prohibition my mother gave voice to that July in Miami Beach. Only later would I learn that my Aunt Ida, in Cuba, ran away at fifteen with a sailor who wasn't Jewish, causing my Sephardic grandmother to wail and tear at her hair as if her daughter had died. Only later would I see how Abuela looked at me with solemn eyes as I held my little cousin on my lap, this girl who was her great-grandchild and had been born from yet another taboo union, between her grandson and a brown Costa Rican woman. Only later would I see how Abuela kept looking with those solemn eyes when the little girl, my cousin, brown like her mother, rose from my lap and I smoothed out the wrinkles left on my silk dress. Only later would I learn from my Aunt Irene, on my mother's side of the family, who grew up in Agramonte, a small town in the Cuban countryside, that she'd been shipped off to Havana when her parents, my great-grandparents, the only Jews in the town, discovered that her flirtation with a local boy was getting "too serious." Only later would I understand how we were Cubans, yes, how we spoke Spanish, yes, and ate black beans, and got nostalgic for Cuba in Miami Beach, and how, yes, we'd have wound up in Hitler's ovens had we not been saved by Cuba, but how, nevertheless, our belonging to the Jewish tribe made it impossible for that whole world that had nourished us, given us life, to have any place in our longing, our desire, our hunger to drink from tongues and bodies that hadn't been branded by the yellow star. Or if we dared—as my aunt had dared—to welcome those tongues and bodies with our own tongues and bodies, it was at the cost of bringing to the Jewish tribe unbearable suffering, grief, a loss so deep it was unto death. Only later would I understand why I claimed a Latina identity so hesitantly, with such excruciating self-hatred, fearing I didn't deserve the love or respect of those Chicanas and Puertorriqueñas and Cubanas who accepted me, who claimed me as one of their own, when I felt unworthy, because I knew, knew it in the heaviness of my heart, that I'd been brought up not to get too close to their men, to stick to "my own kind."

I'd planned to disobey my mother and keep meeting the Puerto Rican boy, somehow, secretly, when we returned to New York at the end of that July vacation in Miami Beach. In his hand I'd slipped a folded piece of paper with my name and address and phone number so he'd find me, so he'd come for me from Spanish Harlem. So he'd take me away from the Ashkenazi Jewish neighborhood in Forest Hills to which my father, a dark, curly-haired Sephardic Jew who was constantly being told *he looked Puerto Rican*, had moved us. Had moved me, the moment I'd entered my teens, trying to keep me safe from the Latino boys and black boys who were being bused into schools in our old Queens neighborhood.

But the Puerto Rican boy never phoned, never showed up in Forest Hills looking for me.

Maybe Mami was right: the Puerto Rican boy wanted one thing and must have realized it would cost too much time and effort to get it from me.

Regardless, the lessons my mother taught me stuck. I became cautious. I became one of those women who waited and waited for that good man to come along.

a sephardi air

....

I grew up within my mother's Ashkenazi family, hearing Yiddish, eating gefilte fish, and adoring my Russian-born grandfather, my Zayde, who had pale green eyes and spoke so softly you could barely hear him. And yet, always, I was reminded by my mother's family how much I resembled my father's Sephardi family. It wasn't only my dark curly hair, Frida Kahlo eyebrows, and large brown eyes that made me more like *el lado turco* (the Turkish side). I was told that my temperament—a strong will, a fierce rage that came from a source I couldn't begin to fathom, and an inability to forgive those who'd wronged me—was a Sephardi temperament. I learned early to believe the Ashkenazim were logical, rational, reasonable, and modern, and Sephardim were moody, irrational, hard-headed, passionate, and fixed in their ways. What's more, I learned that no amount of time spent with my Ashkenazi family would ever rid me of the Sephardi body and soul I'd inherited from the *turcos*.

If I angered Mami, she'd yell, as if uttering a curse, *"¡Eres igualita a tu padre!"* (You're just like your father). But when we were happy, she'd sometimes run her thin fingers through the curls in my hair—her own hair was Indian straight—or watch me gazing into the mirror and say, *"Tienes un aire sefardí, una cosa sefardí muy bonita"* (You have a Sephardi air about you, something Sephardi that's very beautiful). In those moments of affection shaded with detachment, Mami recognized that she'd given birth to a female creature unlike herself, a young woman in whom she saw but little of her own image.

In 1956, in Cuba, the union of my mother, the daughter of *polacos*, and my father, the son of *turcos*, was viewed as practically an intermarriage by both sides of the family. The Ashkenazi and Sephardi communities that put down roots in Cuba in the 1920s had remained apart. They prayed in separate synagogues, lived in separate neighborhoods in Havana, and settled in different regions of Cuba. Baba, hearing of my mother's plans to marry Albertico Behar, had despaired, "But how will we talk to his parents? They don't speak Yiddish!" Spanish, for my maternal grandparents, was the language of the *goyim,* but for my paternal grandparents it was precisely the language of their Jewishness, a thread that wound its way back to Ladino, the fifteenth-century Spanish that Sephardim wrote with Hebrew letters. Little did Baba imagine that a few years later, with the coming of the Revolution, the entire family would depart for the United States, where both Yiddish and Ladino would be lost to new generations and the only language of our diasporic history that would remain with us would be Spanish.

Mami was very close to her Ashkenazi family. I had less contact with my Sephardi family, who resettled in Canarsie, in Brooklyn, after leaving Cuba. Papi, ashamed of his family's poverty in Cuba, drew away from his parents and the Cuban Sephardi community. He was ambitious, and there were more opportunities, both in Havana and later in New York City, to rise into the middle class through Ashkenazi business contacts. Yet he'd always be the *turco* in that world, just as he was in my mother's family.

Although my father was too charming to have ever been an outcast, I saw how he was treated as "other" in the Ashkenazi settings where he tried to make something of himself. I sympathized with him. I too had been marked as *turca* and hence as different within my Ashkenazi family. But even as I understood how he and I were alike, I didn't feel secure around Papi because I feared him. During my adolescent years and after, he was a stern authoritarian father, who regarded me not as his ally but as an overly independent feminist who threatened his power. Praise from his lips for any of my achievements was rare. Criticism and sudden rages that struck like a lightning bolt were the norm. My Sephardi identity came from my father—and it came hesitantly as I was growing into womanhood, without the tenderness I so needed and that would have given me the confidence not to doubt myself at every step.

The stories I heard about my Sephardi family were told by my Ashkenazi family and, therefore, filtered through a lens that was exoticizing, even racist. The story most often told to illustrate how strange were those *turcos* was the tale of my brother's name. When Mori was born in 1959, the year of the Cuban Revolution, my mother, honoring her father's wish, decided to name him Morris to honor the memory of a brother of her father's named Mordechai who'd been killed by the Nazis.

Abuelo and Abuela arrived at the hospital and were enraged to learn that she'd already named the boy. *"¡Este niño es nuestro, nos pertenece a nosotros!"* (This child is ours, he belongs to us), they exclaimed.

Furious in turn, Mami told her in-laws that the child had come from her body and she was honoring a wish of her father's. Abuelo and Abuela, convinced of their rights and deeply hurt, said to her, "But we let you name your first child to honor your side of the family. This second child belongs to us. And we want you to name him Isaac." Mami was doubly shocked. How could a child "belong" to its grandparents rather than to its own mother? And how could a child be named after a living relative?

"Isaac? Name him Isaac? But you're alive! We can't name him Isaac."

And Abuelo replied, "Yes, I'm alive, and I want the boy named after me."

Abuelo was a distinguished-looking man, lean, with a steady gaze and a handsome smile, even though in Cuba he didn't advance beyond being a street peddler and in New York he was employed at Goodman's Matzoh as a factory worker. Abuela had beautiful and pensive dark eyes. Her parents sent her to Cuba on the promise of an arranged marriage, but by the time she arrived her betrothed had married another woman. She played the oud, which she'd brought with her from Turkey, and sang melancholy Sephardi ballads. According to family legend, that was how she attracted the attention of my grandfather. They were both from Silivrí, a small town near Istanbul, and had attended French schools in Turkey before immigrating to Cuba. Abuela was named Rebeca, the same as my mother, which was perhaps why she and Abuelo weren't concerned that her name would be lost.

Mami, holding to the Ashkenazi custom that names are given to newborn children to honor the dead rather than to give joy to the living, refused to change her mind. Finally, she compromised and agreed to name her son Morris Isaac. This compromise, however, failed to placate Abuelo and Abuela, who announced they wouldn't attend the *bris*, the circumcision ceremony, unless the boy was renamed Isaac Morris. As the day drew near and the tensions mounted between my mother and father, Baba and Zayde thought to ask their neighbor Rabbi Gambach, a Sephardi from Turkey, to talk sense into Abuelo and Abuela. They greatly respected Gambach, and he managed to persuade them that, even if Isaac were my brother's middle name, El Abuelo Isaac would be honored just the same. They attended the *bris*, and a semblance of family peace and unity was restored.

Why is it, then, that in telling this story I want to claim the grief and loss of my Sephardi grandparents? I know I would've been beyond furious had my in-laws tried to name my son. But I see now that Abuelo and Abuela were talked into an arrangement that gave their traditions and their memory a secondary place within the family, just as at Passover we always went to their house for the second rather than the first seder.

I'll never forget those second-day Passover seders held at their apartment in Canarsie, never forget the foods Abuela cooked, the tartness of the egg-lemon soup, the delicate taste of the grape leaves stuffed with rice and pine nuts, the gentle crunch of the leek-and-walnut patties, never forget Abuelo telling the story of the expulsion from Egypt with all the drama of an opera. Abuelo's Spanish, Abuela's Spanish, what glorious Spanish they spoke. It was Spanish that could not be learned in any school. Their Spanish made you think of gardens filled with pomegranates, yellow canaries singing in gilded cages on sunny afternoons. It was a gift from my stubborn ancestors, this Spanish for which I had no name when I was a girl, not knowing yet that it was an old Spanish they spoke, a Spanish taken out of Spain many centuries ago. How I would love to hear their voices again, to hear one more time my Abuela calling me, with so much gaiety, not Ruth or Ruti but Rutica; even to hear, one more time, the sadness in Abuelo's voice when he called my brother simply "Mori," for we found "Morris" too stuffy to use in daily life. Mori with the accent on the *o* is how we pronounce my brother's name, but if you place the accent on the *i* it becomes *morí*, which in Spanish means "I died."

We've never once called my brother "Isaac." We never once gave Abuelo that joy in life, and we still deny it to him in death. Isaac is gone from us, as surely and as bitterly as the lover who sings his farewell in the old Sephardi ballad and never again returns.

12/31 - 1929

Baba as a young woman in Havana, 1929.
Photographer unknown.

When I was coming of age in New York in the early 1970s, my family was still struggling to make ends meet. Practical people who sold fabric, envelopes, and shoes, they worried about my dreamy-eyed ways.

The only activity I enjoyed was reading novels and books of philosophy and history, all of which struck them as a waste of time. After I told the family I hoped to become a scholar and writer, they started to become truly concerned about me. To my gregarious, joke-telling, salsa-dancing family, my desire to read books day and night, in utter silence, seemed a lonely, sad, and gloomy pursuit.

"That's silly. If you're so smart, you should be a lawyer or a doctor," said my Uncle Bill, the *americano* in the family. Or even, "Why work so hard? Stay home—a man will come along and marry you." That's what my father hoped.

The sole dissenting voice was that of Baba, my maternal grandmother. "Let her be a scholar and a writer, if she wants to be," Baba told the others. "She takes after my father, her great-grandfather."

Baba had arrived in Cuba from Poland in 1927. Like other Jews who settled on the island in that era, she married and raised her three children in Cuba and never had any intention of leaving. But after Fidel Castro came to power, the loss of her livelihood forced her to immigrate again, to the United States, with the rest of my extended family.

As an immigrant twice over, Baba worked hard. In Cuba, together with my Zayde, she sold lace in their tiny shop on Calle Aguacate in La Habana Vieja, which had cost them years of effort to establish and was taken from them after the Revolution. Afterward, in New York, she and Zayde sold fabric, but as employees at a rundown store belonging to another Jew from Cuba, located under the rattling elevated train in Jamaica, Queens. They worked six days a week but never looked shabby. Zayde had a beautiful head of white hair and always wore a suit and tie. Baba always wore a dress, stockings, and high-heeled shoes. On Saturday afternoons, I enjoyed helping them. I felt very grown up wearing scissors hanging from a string like a necklace, as Baba did, though I wasn't permitted to cut any fabric. She went home at the end of the day with a piercing headache, but she loved to read and to learn, and in the evening she took English courses at the local high school. An insomniac, at night she read the Yiddish newspaper, the *Forverts*, and she kept books by Sholem Aleichem, Isaac Bashevis Singer, and other great Yiddish writers at her bedside. As the years passed and she got better at English, she also read the novels of Danielle Steel.

When they retired, Baba and Zayde moved to Miami Beach. After Zayde died, I visited Baba frequently and would see her sitting up in bed, in the middle of the night, reading from a handwritten Yiddish text. She laughed out loud as she read. Sometimes, though, tears came to her eyes.

"*¿Qué estás leyendo?*" I asked her.

She replied, in English, "The Book." She turned away mysteriously and hid the text under the sheets. She had borrowed The Book, she told me; it was not hers to keep.

After much insistence on my part, I learned that The Book was an unpublished memoir written by her father, my great-grandfather. He'd been the first in my mother's family to arrive in Cuba, in 1925. He worked as a kosher butcher, a cantor, and a street peddler to save enough money to bring over the one child who'd help him get the rest of the family out of Poland: Baba. The eldest of the seven, Baba had begged to follow him to Cuba instead of her brother Moshe, the second child. Though a woman, she promised not to disappoint him. With her drab brown hair and hazy brown eyes, she didn't think herself beautiful like her blonde and blue-eyed mother, but she knew she was smart and determined. She found it boring to be among women who, as she often put it, were weak-willed and "drowned in a glass of water."

Baba's dream was to become a cabaret singer in Cuba. But in 1929, two years after arriving, she married Zayde, after having worked as a salesgirl in his store in Artemisa, on the outskirts of Havana. For five years they scrimped and saved, pooling all their resources with my great-grandfather's to bring my great-grandmother and my great-aunts and great-uncles to safety in Cuba. And just in the nick of time—it was 1934, the eve of the Holocaust, when they set foot in the tropics. Hitler was being named Führer. They would've perished, as did all the family who stayed in Poland.

SEEING HIS WIFE AND YOUNGER CHILDREN again after being separated for nine years, my great-grandfather was so overwhelmed that the story he wanted to tell poured out of him. In 1934, the same year the family was reunited, he recorded the family saga in two empty account ledgers.

"The days of my youth were filled with sadness," opens his tale. In Poland, the family lived off the sale of the two pounds of butter that his mother got from their cow each week. His father cut boughs of juniper to use for heating and cooking, filling their house with a thick smoke. He had no patience for children who couldn't manage on their own. In my great-grandfather's words, "My father believed that a child who could already walk and talk should be making his own way and satisfying his own needs."

My great-grandfather wrote his story while the family was living in Agramonte, a town with a large sugar mill and a strong West African heritage, famous for its reverence of Saint Lazarus, known in the Afro-Cuban pantheon as Babalu-Ayé, a deity who heals the sick and infirm.

But it was as if my great-grandfather never arrived in Cuba.

He didn't write about the long sea journey, or what it felt like to arrive in the tropics in woolen clothing, or how a mango tasted, or how the drums sounded as they played late into the night, calling forth the spirit of Babalu-Ayé. He clung to a lost world in Yiddish, writing about his impoverished youth, his refusal of an arranged marriage, his love for my great-grandmother, and the hardships of their early married years during World War I. He was a dark-haired wisp of a man, with glasses too big for his face, while my great-grandmother was voluptuous. In the old photographs, she towers over him, her arm squeezing his waist, as if he were too frail to hold himself up. Deeply religious, my great-grandfather didn't impose his orthodox beliefs on his children and grandchildren, but he longed for a life of greater Jewish spirituality than was possible in Cuba. In 1948 he and my great-grandmother moved to the newly founded Israel.

In the 1960s, our family left Cuba. The Book fell into the hands of my Great-uncle Gershom. This wasn't surprising; he'd done well for himself, both in Cuba and in Miami, and reigned over the family as a respected godfather. Baba was the eldest, but she looked up to her brother because he was wealthy as well as witty. She and Zayde never figured out the mystery of making money.

"Gershom, please lend me Papá's book again," I heard her say during a family gathering. She spoke, I thought, in much too timid and beseeching a voice. I noticed that Gershom lent her The Book very reluctantly and reminded her he wanted it back.

Several years passed, and in 1996 I was in Miami for five months on a research grant, accompanied by David and our son, Gabriel, who was ten years old at the time. Every afternoon I'd visit Baba and we'd read The Book in her kitchen.

We sat across from each other on yellow wooden chairs that matched the yellow Formica table that matched the orange and yellow marigold wallpaper. I do not know Yiddish, and Baba and I almost never spoke English to each other. She did what was natural for us: she patiently read my great-grandfather's story aloud, word by word, in Yiddish, then translated everything into Spanish, while I wrote it down. On those afternoons, sunshine seemed to have been invented just to illuminate my great-grandfather's words.

One afternoon the spell was broken. Gershom was knocking on the door.

I pulled my grandmother aside. "Don't give The Book back to him," I whispered. Gershom had allowed Baba to hold on to both volumes of The Book for a few months, and I didn't want her to lose them again.

"How can I not return The Book?" Baba asked.

"Hide The Book and tell him you can't find it."

My grandmother was stunned but did as I asked.

When Gershom entered, the first thing he said was, "Give me The Book, Esther."

She replied, "I'm not sure where I put it. I'll look for it later. Sit down, I made cookies."

Then she used the Spanish pun that all the old Yiddish folks from Cuba adored. "*¿Te quiere?*" she asked, which literally means "Does she or he love you?" but the word *té* with an accent on the *e* means "tea" rather than "you." So the question, a double-entendre, can also be interpreted as, "You want tea?"

Gershom said yes to cookies and tea that day, and for many days afterward.

IN THIS WAY, BABA HELD ON TO THE BOOK for the last four years of her life. I was proud of our conspiracy. Mine was a skewed calculation, to be sure, but I justified our plotting as a fair distribution of the things of the world. Gershom had money and unwavering self-confidence. We would have The Book.

Not long after Baba died, I retrieved The Book from its hiding place under her nightstand. As soon as it was in my hands, I rushed it home as though it were looted treasure. I buried it in my fireproof file cabinet, where I also keep old family pictures and other memorabilia from Cuba.

Gershom lived another two years after Baba's death. When one of my mother's Israeli cousins learned I had The Book, she demanded I return it to him. "What do you want it for?" she hissed. "You don't even know Yiddish."

She was right, and yet I didn't give it to him. I discovered that I'm as greedy about wanting The Book all to myself as Gershom was. No—worse than Gershom. In my defense, let me say that I've made copies of The Book for everyone in my family. But I've clung to the original handwritten text.

Just as Jacob stole Esau's birthright with the complicity of his mother, Baba stole The Book from her brother to pass it on to me. I'm glad we were such good thieves. Wanting to be a scholar and a writer wasn't easy in my family. Lacking their encouragement left within me a deep well of insecurity. Baba understood the challenges facing me.

In my darkest hour, when I can't be sure if the years of reading and learning have taught me anything, when I can't be sure if my writing is going well, I draw strength from my great-grandfather and marvel at how he found the presence of mind to sit in a town in Cuba, surrounded by sugarcane, and write about a Polish Jewish world that was about to vanish. Now that I'm in possession of The Book, I realize I'm not alone. My desire to study and to write didn't come out of thin air. I'm the bearer of an *herencia*, an inheritance, that I must never forsake.

A day may yet come when I'll learn Yiddish and be able to read The Book in the original. But if that day never comes, I won't let go of those two account ledgers. The Book is my shield. My talisman. My most precious ruby. I jealously guard it and keep it stored away, under lock and key. Hidden from others—even from myself.

Note: Some names have been changed to protect the privacy of family members.

Balcony in Havana. Left to right:
Miguel, Mami, Zayde, and Ruth.
1958. Photographer unknown.

the day i cried at
starbucks on lincoln road

....

It could've been blissful, my four-month visit to Miami Beach in 2009 to carry out research, teach, and escape the dreariness of a Michigan winter. I was on my own. David was teaching in Michigan and Gabriel had already graduated from NYU and was living in Brooklyn. I'd rented an apartment in a historic Art Deco building a block from the ocean. As soon as I got organized, I planned to invite my Uncle Miguel and Aunt Reina and their children and grandchildren, as well as my mother's cousin Anna, for Sunday brunch so they could admire the lovely view.

But in February, a gorgeous time of the year in Miami, an essay I'd published in *Hadassah Magazine* demolished my family plans.

Originally I'd given the piece an innocuous title, "The Yiddish Book from Cuba." I told the story of how, with Baba's help, I'd come into the possession of my great-grandfather's handwritten memoir. "I'm glad we were such good thieves," I'd written.

The editor at *Hadassah Magazine* saw the dramatic potential of this line and changed the title of my essay to "Such Good Thieves." I feared the new title would be misunderstood and read as a statement of fact by my family and tried to change it back to the old one. But it was too late. The magazine had already gone to press.

It was my first time publishing in *Hadassah Magazine*. Just before her death, Baba had made me a life member of Hadassah, a Jewish women's organization in which she'd been active after retiring and settling in Miami Beach. I thought it would be nice to honor her by publishing my essay in the organization's widely circulated magazine.

What I hadn't anticipated was that "widely circulated" meant that my family, as well as many friends of my family who form part of the Cuban Jewish immigrant circle, saw the essay. Worst of all, they actually read it. And they hated it.

Among those who hated it most was my Uncle Miguel.

He phoned me and said, "Can you meet me at the Starbucks on Lincoln Road tomorrow morning?"

"Sure, okay."

"Eleven o'clock. I've got to talk to you about your article in *Hadassah Magazine.*"

My uncle was asking me to meet him at Starbucks? I didn't remember any occasion when I'd been alone with him. My Aunt Reina was always by his side. Often their three children and their spouses and grandchildren were also around. They're a tight-knit family and live within a few blocks of each other in Miami Beach.

Miguel was the baby; my Aunt Sylvia was ten and my mother was eight when he was born. The family had just moved to Havana from Agramonte. By a stroke of good fortune, Zayde had won 5,000 pesos in the Cuban lottery in 1944. With that money he and Baba were able to leave the countryside and buy their lace shop on Calle Aguacate.

When I was born, Miguel was twelve—too young to be an uncle.

There's a yellowed photograph I keep in a frame above my desk in Michigan. I'm a year old, decked out in a sailor dress and perched on Zayde's lap in the balcony of our old apartment in La Habana. Mami sits in the rocking chair next to us. Miguel balances on the arm of Mami's chair. In his short-sleeved shirt and tailored pants, he's no longer a boy, but neither is he yet a man.

Afterward, when we all left Cuba and settled in the United States, I felt that my Uncle Miguel didn't approve of the kind of woman I'd become—too intellectual, too independent, too liberal. I was married and a mother, yet I traveled by myself on return journeys to Cuba, a place we weren't supposed to go back to.

"I didn't realize there was a Starbucks on Lincoln Road," I say.

"It's there. You'll find it."

I hear a jittery edge to his voice.

The next morning, a Sunday, I'm up early and take a walk on the beach, enjoying the ocean's calm, the breeze like silk against my skin. The sun warms my shoulders. I feel lucky. It's icy back in Michigan.

But I don't linger. I want to be punctual for my appointment with Miguel. My parking spot turns out to be around the corner from the Starbucks I'd never noticed. All the tables outside are taken, so I claim a table inside, next to the window. I toss the leftover paper cups and wipe the table with a napkin. Then I busy myself deleting spam on my BlackBerry.

The phone rings.

"Are you there?"

"Yes, but no rush. Take your time."

"I'll be there soon. I just wanted to be sure you were there."

Miguel arrives, and our cheeks brush against each other as we quickly kiss hello. It stuns me to think he's in his mid-sixties. My young uncle. His cheeks are redder, his thinning hair grayer.

"What do you want to drink?" he asks.

"I'll take an iced tea."

"Iced tea in the morning? Not coffee?"

"I don't drink coffee in the morning. It gives me migraines."

Miguel seems to frown and I wonder if my reply reinforces his idea of me as an oddball.

He returns and places the cup in front of me. "It's passion fruit tea. Is that okay?"

"Thanks, that's great."

He's gotten a large coffee for himself. He reaches into his shirt pocket and unfolds a ragged photocopy of my essay.

I wince when I see it.

"You're ready?" Miguel says.

"Sure, shoot."

I look at his copy stabbed with underlining and highlighting. It's almost illegible.

"Here, at the beginning, you say you're a scholar and that's why you deserved to inherit The Book my grandfather wrote. But what's a scholar? A scholar's somebody who knows a lot about a subject. I'm an accountant because I know a lot about accounting. I'm a scholar too. I'm a scholar of accounting. So I should have The Book. Are you going to give it to me?"

Before I can think of how to reply, he takes a pen from his shirt pocket and circles a word that's already been circled.

"This, I really hated. 'Tiny.' Why'd you use that word?"

"You mean my referring to Baba and Zayde's lace store in Havana as tiny?"

"It wasn't tiny. It wasn't any smaller than the other stores owned by Jews on Calle Aguacate."

"But I'm not comparing their store to anybody else's store. I'm just saying *their* store was tiny. That's what I always heard."

"How do you know? You're not old enough to remember. I remember. I was there. I worked with them in the store. And then Castro came and took it away."

"Would you have preferred if I'd said 'small' instead of 'tiny'?"

"Maybe. 'Tiny' makes their store sound poor—like it was nothing. Like they were nobody."

"I'm sorry. I didn't realize you could read so much into the word 'tiny.' I was just saying their store was a very small store."

"You're supposed to be a writer, but you don't seem to think about the meaning of the words you're using."

I glance out the window, enviously taking in the profane beauty of a Sunday on Lincoln Road: translucent morning light, swaying palm trees, people strolling along the pedestrian boulevard, looking marvelously carefree, clasping their children, their exotic dogs, their trophy shopping bags, their lovers.

With his pen Miguel recircles another word.

"Then you say that Baba worked at a 'rundown store' when we came to New York. It wasn't rundown. Do you know whose store that was? It belonged to Jacobo. He was a friend of the family. You think he'd like you saying his store was 'rundown'? That's not a nice thing to say."

"But the store *was* rundown! That I do remember. I used to go help Baba and Zayde on Saturdays. I remember Gem Fabrics. I remember how the elevated train rattled above the store. I remember how Baba wore scissors tied on a string around her neck, the scissors for cutting fabric."

"It was a good store. Jacobo was very nice to give them jobs. I worked there too. I worked very hard. I had to carry packages to the storeroom. We didn't have any money and I had to help out. You probably don't know that."

I envision Miguel at seventeen, newly arrived from Cuba, scarcely able to speak English, and having to spend his days lugging bundles and bolts of fabric, his eyes itchy from the dust, his hands sore and calloused. In those days he lived with Baba and Zayde in their one-bedroom apartment in Queens, three flights below our apartment, and before dinner, as was the custom in Cuba, he'd take a shower. I remember him in a big bath towel as he sprang from the bathroom to the bedroom, leaving a trail of talcum powder, white as glistening sand.

Miguel skims the next couple of lines. Fortunately, he doesn't see anything offensive. Then his pen stops at the point where I state that The Book fell into the hands of my Great-uncle Gershom. Attacking the line with a glob of black ink, he reads my own words aloud to me: "This wasn't surprising; he'd done well for himself, both in Cuba and Miami, and reigned over the family as a respected godfather."

"This is horrible. How could you call him a 'godfather'? A godfather is a mafioso, someone who kills others to get what he wants."

"I wasn't using the word that way! I was thinking of *padrino* in the Cuban or Latin American sense—as the patriarch, the head of the family."

"You said 'godfather.' You really hurt Anna's feelings with that word."

Anna, my second cousin, is Gershom's only surviving child. She too lives in Miami Beach but refrained from calling or meeting me in person. Instead she sent me an email to let me know how upset she was about my essay. She commanded me never to write about her father again. "Let him rest in peace," she insisted. But at the end of the email she wrote, "I still love you." I wasn't sure she meant it, though. She later told other members of the family that she doesn't want to see me again.

I feel bad about hurting Anna's feelings. My heart has always gone out to her. Her younger brother died of leukemia in Cuba, and while he was dying, no one told her what was going on. I've written about searching for his Jewish grave in Cuba, and though I've done so in the most caring way I could, she told me in her email that she didn't want me to write about her brother anymore either.

Miguel shakes his head. "Anna didn't want her children to see your essay. She knew they'd be angry. But someone saw it in California and sent it to her daughter."

Anna also has two sons. I've always gotten along well with them, especially her younger son, who has an artistic soul and bears the namesake of her brother. Maybe he too has vowed not to speak to me anymore.

But what can I do about the fact that in Cuba, and in our Cuban Jewish enclave, Gershom *was* the godfather of the family? We all depended on his largesse. It was Gershom who gave my newlywed father, a Sephardic Jew who'd grown up in a tenement near the Port of Havana, an accounting job at his store so he could properly support my mother, who fell pregnant (with me) the instant she married. It was Gershom who sold one of his condominiums to Baba and Zayde when they headed south to Miami Beach for their final years of sunshine. It was Gershom who supported his younger brother, Jaime, a dreamer and a Socialist, and his four nieces on Kibbutz Gaash in Israel.

Did I mean to suggest Gershom was evil because he was a man of means and knew that he was? Not for a moment. I found him to be very charming and we got along well. He was forever asking why I didn't go dig up something in Israel. I'd tell him I wasn't an archaeologist, and he'd say that didn't matter. He thought it was great that I loved doing research, and he hoped I'd write one day about the history of the Jews of Cuba. Once, when I was visiting Miami, he led me on a wild-goose chase for supposedly important documents that we tracked down in some old suitcases in a friend's warehouse. The "documents" turned out to be mostly clippings from the social pages of Miami newspapers that had gotten waterlogged in a flood and turned to mush. We had a roller-coaster adventure searching for them all over the city, with Gershom bringing his Cadillac to a full stop on the highway several times to be able to read the exit signs. It was a wonder we didn't end up in a car crash. But I wasn't afraid. Gershom's desire to help me in my work was so sincere that I knew an angel was watching over us.

I could understand why his daughter and grandchildren would find my portrait of him in my essay unbecoming. They'd depict Gershom as the generous philanthropist of the family. Being at a distance, and coming from the poorer side, I picked up on the resentment that the recipients of his largesse, particularly my father and grandfather, came to feel; the way Baba seemed to admire her brother more than her husband, my beloved Zayde; the way Mami seemed not to notice that Papi still carried wounds from the days he'd been treated by Gershom as merely a poor *turco*, and that was the reason he tried so hard to demand obedience from my mother, Mori, and me, and ruled in our house with both harshness and self-doubt, a heartbroken dictator. A generation later, I hadn't escaped the "hidden injuries of class." I was ashamed of my humble origins. In a world where worth is measured by wealth, those closest to me had not been able to achieve enough. "Empty pockets don't ever make the grade," as Billie Holiday sang so wrenchingly. I'd been a fool to think I could make it up to Zayde and Papi with my writing.

Miguel, I soon learned, had no sympathy for my position. "Did it ever occur to you that maybe Gershom had The Book for a reason? He was the eldest son. Maybe his father wanted him to have it."

"I really don't think so. Baba was the eldest child."

"But you don't know for sure."

"No, I don't."

"And so you decided to turn your grandmother—my mother—into a thief, so you could get The Book for yourself."

"I didn't force Baba to do anything. I suggested that she keep The Book, but she was free to do whatever she wanted."

"She loved you so much she would've done anything for you."

"And I would've done anything for her. I adored Baba."

"Then why did you stain her name?"

"I didn't stain her name."

"You did. You say she was a 'good thief.' There's one thing my father always said: the most important possession a person has in life is his name. If you ruin that, you ruin everything."

"Miguel, please! I used 'thief' as a metaphor."

"Look, what I think you forget is that Baba didn't belong just to you. She was also my mother. She was also my children's grandmother. We all loved her—not just you."

These words inexplicably bring tears to my eyes.

Miguel smiles. "Good," he says. "It's good you're crying."

He keeps his gaze on me and I feel so humiliated I lower my head. When I finally look up, I see a long line of people waiting to be served at the counter. How I wish I could dissolve into that crowd and never be heard from again.

But the knife cuts deeper. "You're the kind of scholar who'd do anything to get the documents you want, aren't you? What would you think if I called your university in Michigan and told them you stole The Book from your great-uncle because you thought you had a right to it? And you don't even read Yiddish! So why are you keeping it?"

"Miguel, I was the only one who ever cared about the history of the family. So what if I have the original? You can read the story. It's all been translated."

"What if I want to be the one who's got the original? Will you give The Book to me? Or do I have to go steal it out of your file cabinet?"

I want to say, "Sure, I'll give you The Book if you want it so badly." Those words refuse to come out of my mouth. As I take the last sip of my passion fruit tea, I'm convinced I'm the lowest of the low. I expect Miguel to rip up my essay before my eyes. But he folds it neatly, this writing of mine to which he'd devoted Talmudic attention, and stuffs it back into his shirt pocket. We say goodbye politely, walking our separate ways on Lincoln Road.

The days pass. I never miss a morning's walk on the beach.

I don't hear from Miguel or my Aunt Reina. Nor do I phone them.

Two of my mother's cousins come for a visit in April, and they meet me for lunch on Lincoln Road. They tell me about the family dinner at Little Havana Restaurant. Anna refuses to go if I'm going, and they think Miguel and Reina feel the same way. Better not to rock the boat, they say. And again I feel like the leper of the family.

Passover, the Jewish remembrance of our freedom from slavery, comes and goes. I remain in exile—unworthy of a place at the seder table of my Miami family. Fortunately, I'm invited to the home of the parents of a friend for Passover, so I'm not alone. Still, I feel sad that the one and only time I'm in Miami for the holiday I find myself bereft of kin.

Near the end of my time in Miami Beach, in early May, I'm driving on the Venetian causeway that leads back to my rental apartment and I catch a fleeting glimpse of Miguel and Reina taking a sunset walk.

Evenings are growing hot already. I watch Miguel wipe his brow with a tissue. Reina stands next to him patiently. They've been sweethearts since she was thirteen and he was fifteen in Cuba. I hope they'll always be blessed, my young uncle, my affable aunt, who loves to sing and is the life of every party. In the past, I would've stopped the car and turned back to greet them, gone home with them. But I feel I should crawl away. I'm a stranger.

Then it's time to pack my bags and return to Michigan, where a cold spring awaits me. Before I close the door of the Art Deco apartment, I look back at the view—the infinite sky, the turquoise ocean, so beautiful, and so lonely.

At that moment, I don't yet know that eventually my Uncle Miguel will forgive me and I will be welcomed again into the warmth of his and Reina's home. I don't yet know that later, much later, even my cousin Anna will take me back as family. At that moment, when I feel certain my sins are too great to ever be forgiven, I'm grateful the sky and the ocean still love me.

Note: Some names have been changed to protect the privacy of family members.

a tango for gabriel

....

In his junior year in high school, my son, Gabriel, was asked to produce a chase scene as an assignment for his filmmaking class. He made a short movie that he titled *Run*.

Acting as the protagonist, Gabriel plays a bored student falling asleep at his school desk. He enters into a dream state and leaves the classroom and roams through the hallways, finding an open locker. Peering inside, he sees a jacket. He reaches into the pocket, discovers a wallet, and decides to snatch it. Just as he's sneaking the wallet into his pocket, the friend he's stealing it from catches him in the act. The chase scene ensues. Both young men run through the school hallways at a dizzying pace. Gabriel runs down a long flight of stairs with his friend behind him. He makes a dramatic leap over the banister and, landing safely, sprints out the door. But he falls as he gets outside. The betrayed friend, a huge guy, pulls Gabriel up by his collar and punches him in the nose. The screen fades to black. Gabriel awakens in his classroom. The film ends as it began, with him bored at his desk, hypnotically fiddling with a pencil.

My son represented himself as an athlete: limber, dashing, quick-jumping. The film is about the attraction of speed. It's about sitting still at a desk but wanting to run. As Gabriel's mother, I noticed that in the shots where he was racing down the stairs, his legs weren't working symmetrically—he was favoring his left leg. But I didn't say anything.

Gabriel was running—that was all that mattered. He'd been able to make a film called *Run* and run in it himself.

It was a Saturday night when Gabriel finished editing *Run* on my computer at the university. I recall the date: March 29, 2003. Gabriel was sixteen and a half. The next day, in the afternoon, he had his weekly Sunday basketball game. He was on a recreational team, nothing too competitive, with his high school friends. During most of the season, he'd hung back, taking a lot of water breaks, playing cautiously. He refrained from putting his whole self into the game. I watched his lackluster behavior with sorrow, remembering what a strong, passionate athlete he'd been before he turned twelve. My sorrow turned to anger, as it always did, as I thought about the athlete he should have been. But the good thing, I told myself, was that he was back in the game and that he could be with his friends.

On that Sunday, March 30, he played differently, more confidently, perhaps because he'd just completed *Run*. He stayed on the court. He didn't take a water break. He scored a basket, his first of the season. He was exhilarated. He got into place to block an opponent. Then it happened. He jumped, hyperextended while in the air, and fell to the floor, landing on his stomach. I closed my eyes and prayed that what I feared hadn't come to pass. When I looked again, Gabriel was pounding the floor with his fists.

David and I rushed over. The first thing Gabriel said as we approached was, "Get me some crutches." He couldn't get up. The game wasn't over yet. A few teammates helped him hop to the bench on the sidelines. The game continued with Gabriel watching quietly. I stayed next to him. After a while, he told me to go back to the other side of the gym.

When the game ended, David returned with the crutches he'd gone home to find. We'd saved those crutches, though I'd always intended to give them away. To keep the crutches after they were no longer needed could bring bad luck. But I'd forgotten, and they'd stayed in the closet for four years. The crutches were now too small for Gabriel. He had to stoop forward and hunch his shoulders to walk with them. It hurt to see him on the crutches again.

The day after he finished *Run*, Gabriel was stopped in his tracks. He ran and was caught. Unfortunately, it wasn't a dream. His first effort at making a movie became a premonition, an elegy to his lost speed.

AS A BOY, GABRIEL WAS A STAR ATHLETE. There wasn't a sport he wasn't good at. His peers named him the most athletic boy of their sixth-grade class. He played racquetball with my father, tennis with my father-in-law. His coordination was stunning, his reflexes unfailing. By the age of eleven he was the point guard of his basketball team. He was on the verge of being a promising football player. But soccer was his passion. What made him such a valuable soccer player was his keen strategic sense of where all his teammates were on the field relative to him. He passed the ball so it landed by the toes of his teammates; all they had to do to make a goal was to coax the ball into the net. His feet were winged. In the course of a single game he could score several breakaway goals. I watched in awe. He had the grace of a dancer but shunned my efforts to encourage him to study ballet. He wanted to do the manly thing: play sports.

At first I'd brought a book to read during the soccer games. These games, I felt, were being taken much too seriously by the other parents. But after a while the sheer pleasure of seeing my son exhibit such confidence on the field made it impossible for me to be indifferent. The solidarity among the parents gave me a sense of community. I'd take a seat next to David in our lawn chairs, along with the other parents, as the boys played their weekly, sometimes twice weekly games. I'd get so excited I'd leap up and position myself at the edge of the field, running alongside Gabriel and jumping like a cheerleader when he scored a goal. Bundled in long underwear and a down jacket when it was cold, or wearing a T-shirt and jeans in the heat, there was I, a woman who usually wore tailored skirts and high heels, yelling, "Go Gabriel!" I became what I never thought I'd become: a fervent soccer mom. When the game was over, I enjoyed taking our turn handing out juice boxes and Oreo cookies for snack time. Gabriel, like all the boys, would be drenched in sweat. His face glowed from the joyous release of physical exercise. The parents of his friends often complimented David and me on his skills as a soccer player. "How did two intellectual parents create such an athletic kid?" they'd ask. I feared they were giving Gabriel the evil eye. As it turned out, they were.

David and I weren't athletic, and we made no effort to encourage Gabriel to pursue team sports. David had had severe myopia as a child and wore thick glasses, becoming a bookworm at an early age and developing a stooping posture. I, in turn, broke my femur in a car accident in New York when I was nine and was in a body cast for a year. After emerging from the cast, I used crutches for several months and limped for such a long time that my family feared I'd never walk right again. It took years, many years, for me to trust my legs. As a young woman, I lost my appetite for physical activity, turning to books for comfort and imaginary flights to other worlds.

Building his identity as an athlete, Gabriel set down roots in the town of Ann Arbor. Every time I suggested we move to a warmer climate—I dreamed of Miami Beach and a toasty ocean—Gabriel would veto the idea, begging me not to move until he'd finished high school. Seeing him so at home in the college town where he'd been born and raised, I felt it was time for me to put down roots in Ann Arbor too. As an anthropologist, I'd spent my life postponing the question of where I belonged, doing research as a sanctioned expatriate in Spain and Mexico and later in my own native Cuba. Maybe it was time to finally be an

American. I had a secure job at the University of Michigan. I had a house, a car, and a retirement account.

Gabriel had one dream for when he grew up: to be a scholar-athlete at the University of Michigan and play on their football team. With a native son's pride, he told me, "Mommy, Michigan has the biggest college stadium in the country. Imagine playing for 120,000 people!"

Ann Arbor is a football town where, year after year, on a dozen Saturdays in autumn, the streets fill up with thousands of fans dressed in maize and blue going to watch the game. And I've never even been to a football game. But there was a time, a time for which I now wax nostalgic, when I wanted to be lured to the football stadium, the way I'd been lured to the soccer field—by my son's love for the game. I imagined myself in the future going to every football game, watching my son play, watching sports pave the way for all he hoped to achieve.

My worst fear, as Gabriel grew up, was that he'd hurt one of his legs, as I'd done as a child. I was away when the first injury happened, on the soccer field. On that afternoon in July 1998, I was lecturing at the Getty Center in Los Angeles about the meaning of the millennium. The new century was near, and it called for interpretation. I'd written a book urging all observers to summon their emotions in the act of being witnesses to other people's lives. I described myself as a broken-hearted anthropologist, but I had no idea what broken-heartedness awaited me back in Ann Arbor.

On the phone, just before I was due to fly back to Michigan, David told me not to worry. "We went to the doctor. He said there's no fracture. He has a swollen knee, but it should go away. It's nothing to worry about."

Oh, dear god, but when I saw Gabriel at the airport, I knew something was very wrong with his leg. He had a limp that made him seesaw as he walked. Seeing my son impaired this way brought back horrible memories of my own leg injury. I sensed he would need expert medical attention to determine what had happened. I hated myself for intuitively realizing his knee injury was nothing trivial.

And I was enraged at how the injury had happened. The assistant coach of Gabriel's soccer team had joined the boys during a practice. A librarian who was also a runner, he took the game too seriously. I'd noticed him coolly eyeing Gabriel on the field. He never cheered when Gabriel scored goals for the team. I'd seen him scold Gabriel for missing a throw-in shot, insensitive to the fact that Gabriel was furious at himself for having let the team down. His own son was a poor player. On the day of the practice, while running to get the ball away from Gabriel, he gave Gabriel a fatal kick—brutal enough that Gabriel told me he'd felt the cleats slice into his calves.

He had knocked Gabriel to the ground. Gabriel was hurt so badly he screamed, "Are you trying to kill me?" The head coach reprimanded Gabriel for displaying anger, telling him it had been an accident. Gabriel limped off the field and for the next hour sat on the sidelines while his teammates and the two coaches kept playing. He was a good sport and waited, didn't tell them how excruciating was the pain. No apology was given by either coach. Not long afterward, the coach who'd injured Gabriel left town.

In those days Gabriel had straight blond hair. He was lean and sprightly, with long arms and long legs, like his father, and the soft brown trusting eyes of a boy who'd not yet suffered any terrible disappointments. A few days before he entered sixth grade, we headed to the Med Sport facility for an appointment with a doctor on the sports medicine team at the University of Michigan. For over three hours various assistants and associates administered tests, took X-rays, and twisted and turned Gabriel's knee in the strangest ways. When the real doctor came through the door, svelte as a fox and with long prying fingers, he maneuvered Gabriel's knee briskly and delivered the bad news:

Gabriel's left ACL was ruptured, and he'd need surgery to repair the ligament. We scarcely had a moment to take in this diagnosis before he whipped out a colorful anatomical diagram of the knee and explained to us how he'd undertake the surgery. He'd take a piece of tendon from the same leg—either a hamstring or patellar tendon, but he much preferred the patellar tendon—and create a new ligament by running the graft through holes he'd drill into the femur and tibia. Six to eight months of physical therapy would follow. "I'll have your son back on the soccer field by next summer," he announced cheerfully.

I burst into tears, and so did Gabriel. In that instant, we bonded as mother and son, as though my once injured right leg and his now injured left leg were the limbs of a single body. Watching us weep, David didn't know whom to comfort. He tried to put his arm around each of us, but we were inconsolable. The doctor seemed not to notice. Without the surgery, he warned, Gabriel's unstable knee would continually give way and grow weaker. In an ominous tone, he said Gabriel would need to be extremely careful not to have too many "giving-way episodes." He was to avoid all twisting, turning, and jumping sports. One wrong step and his knee might be injured beyond repair. Then he told my son, "Don't dance. Whatever you do, don't dance."

I found myself recoiling from these scare tactics and asked whether he would mind if we got a second opinion. He had no objections and told his secretary to give us a list of other orthopedic surgeons. He recommended especially highly a doctor at Harvard University. So Gabriel and I traveled to Cambridge. This doctor advised that we hold off on surgery until Gabriel was older because of the possibility of damaging his growth plates. He X-rayed Gabriel's wrist and said that at bone-age fourteen, he'd be ready for surgery. Wait two years, he suggested. In the meantime, he urged Gabriel to do physical therapy, bike, and swim to keep strong.

We had two years' reprieve. We found our way to Ann Arbor's Ice

Cube, a gym and a physical therapy center overlooking an enormous ice-skating rink. While exercising, you could watch children taking first steps on the ice, or marvel at the advanced figure skaters doing dance moves in perfect harmony, or catch hockey teams at work on their drills.

Gabriel became a regular at the Cube, doing physical therapy three times a week. He was their youngest patient. The therapist tried to make the routine enjoyable, but the exercises were lonely and boring activities, to be undertaken indoors on machines, without any glimpse of sunshine.

It became wrenching to pass a soccer field, to see kids playing basketball at an outdoor court. Those activities were now forbidden to Gabriel. He never complained or bemoaned his loss, but I'd notice the sorrow clouding his eyes as we drove past and saw the other kids sweating from the strenuous physical activities he loved and once excelled at. My athletic child had developed an invisible disability. He appeared to be normal, but he was not to jump, run, twist, or turn. And he was not to dance. He'd lost the ability to move freely, to move without thinking.

Since I took Gabriel back and forth to the Cube for therapy, I joined the gym and became a regular myself. I ran on the treadmill, pedaled fast on the stationary bike. I was exercising more than I'd ever exercised in my life. Perhaps I imagined that if my legs could grow strong I could help Gabriel to strengthen his legs.

IT WAS AT THAT TIME THAT I STARTED dancing the tango. David wasn't interested, so I went alone. A friend in Michigan had told me about the local tango club, headed by an Argentine woman who'd recovered from a serious leg injury. "I bet you'll love it," she said.

When I was growing up, I'd danced at parties with friends and family, moving my body fluidly, spontaneously, to salsa and cha-cha-cha tunes that were inescapable in our Cuban Jewish immigrant community. But to surrender my will to a man who led me around the floor, to learn steps, to pay attention to each of my movements—that was totally new to me.

Ultimately, my friend was right. I did come to love the tango, though they say you can love the tango, but it doesn't necessarily love you back. That's how it was for me; for years, tango was my greatest unrequited love. I hobbled around the dance floor and was as heavy as furniture that had to be lifted and carried.

Slowly, ever so slowly, I improved. Once I could do basic steps, like walking backward in high-heeled stilettos, keeping my posture and embrace from sagging while being led into moves that made me feel I was about to levitate, tango became an essential form of self-expression. Who could have predicted that in my forties I'd take up this sensual pastime? I'd reached the age when I should've been reading the Kabbalah. Instead, a couple of times a week, I joined a bunch of strangers who patiently tried to balance each other's bodies while listening to the melancholy songs of Buenos Aires.

It was amazing to me to discover the range of men I could dance with as I got better—tall, short, thin, husky, young, old, it didn't matter. I could dance with men, Polish or German, who in another era might have cooperated in my destruction, who would have seen only the Jew in me. I could dance with men, Palestinian and Arab, who in another place might see only the enemy in me. Tango, like yoga, could quell unease, quiet the mind of prejudices and worries, and, with regular practice, bring about peace.

Being led around the dance floor with my eyes closed, as I was advised to do to enter a "tango trance," I was frequently in tears as I thought about the limitations on my son's movements. Tango became a way to tell, without words, the story of my anguish about Gabriel's loss of his athletic gift. It was anguish I carried with me day after day, unable to speak about it because I didn't want to sadden him.

GABRIEL CELEBRATED HIS BAR MITZVAH AND, two months before turning fourteen, had surgery to reconstruct his knee. It was June 2000. He had finished eighth grade. His hair had begun to turn brown and become curly and unruly like mine. He'd grown muscular from the physical therapy.

Local anesthesia was all that was used for the surgery. Gabriel bravely watched the entire operation. After he was wheeled out of the operating room, he was giddy from the drugs they'd given him. "It wasn't so bad, Mommy," he said with a smile. But an hour later, he stumbled getting up to go to the bathroom and became furious at himself. I had to turn away so he wouldn't see me cry.

That afternoon David and I took Gabriel home. We got him settled on the sofa, and every hour I brought him fresh ice packs to bring down the swelling. Seeing him lying around with his bandaged leg, his gaze bleary from the painkillers he was taking, I wondered why we, as a mother and son, had both needed to experience the loss of movement. What kind of destiny was this, that we should know firsthand the terror of being invalids?

Gabriel steadily got better, though the scar was thick and purple. It worried me, but the doctor said it was a keloid and that some people developed them. I calmed down because Gabriel's condition kept improving. He did physical therapy. He got strong. A year later the doctor agreed that he could attend several one-week summer camps: a track camp, a soccer camp, and a basketball camp. Yes, he could join the track team. And, yes, most important of all for Gabriel, he could join the high school football team. In the end, he only practiced with the team; he was called to play briefly, twice, in actual games. But every day he attended football practice after school. He was living his dream—almost.

I loved seeing him trust his body again.

We went to Med Sport regularly for return visits. The doctor, surrounded by an entourage of assistants and therapists, would inspect

Gabriel's knee. Before surgery, the doctor saw his patients in a private examining room, but after surgery, after he'd used his knife, they were all seen publicly in the clinic. Patient after patient, dozens of people, waited at the exam tables.

There was the day the boy to our left, just before Gabriel's turn, received bad news. The doctor said something that made it clear that sports were over for the boy. He wept. His mother stood next to him like a ghost. Then the doctor came to Gabriel's side. Gabriel was doing well. He was still one of the model patients. The doctor patted him on the back. He checked Gabriel's knee, checked his gait. Everything was fine. He could go forward, play sports. We were the lucky ones.

AS GABRIEL AND I WAITED AGAIN in the small exam room with the flickering fluorescent lights, where he'd first been seen when he was twelve, we knew the blessed moment of his recovery had ended. It was April Fool's Day 2003, two days after the basketball game in which he'd played so exuberantly after making his movie, *Run*. Now Gabriel was sixteen going on seventeen. He was expecting bad news and looked sullen as he sat on the exam table, his legs dangling over the edge. Like the first time, we waited for three hours. Finally, the resident entered, a tall, fat-faced man with a buzz cut. He poked and pulled Gabriel's left leg, performed the Lachman test, maneuvering the leg to test for looseness between the tibia and the femur. He said nothing. When he was done, he told us the doctor would come soon. We waited another half hour. At last the doctor sailed in. Not bothering to say hello, he did a two-second exam and confirmed what the resident had whispered in his ear in the hallway.

The two doctors, enormous nightmare figures, towered over Gabriel, who was curled into a ball of worry and shame on the examination table.

"We think you've torn the graft. And the meniscus." The doctor spoke in a flat voice. "We'll do an MRI and see what options you have, but we're certain you're going to need another knee reconstruction. On a revision, I suggest a quadriceps tendon autograft, but let's wait for the MRI." He paused. I expected him to offer a few words of sympathy. Instead he said, "This doesn't happen to us very often."

Cruel doctor's words: it was the boy's fault. Gabriel had botched the fine doctor's handiwork. No explanation was offered of why things had gone wrong.

Hearing the bad news, Gabriel refused to shed even a single tear. I drove him to school and he got out of the car, leaning on his new crutches for support. "Don't cry," he told me, an angry edge to his voice.

The MRI results confirmed that the graft was torn, and so was the posterior horn of the lateral meniscus. But when we returned to the clinic, the doctor didn't discuss options. He offered only one solution: a quadriceps tendon autograft. I'd had time to get on the web and research the various graft possibilities and learned that a reconstruction with a quadriceps tendon autograft was a risky and rarely performed surgery. It left an unsightly scar and weakened the leg from which the tendon was removed.

I challenged the doctor and the resident to justify the need for this surgery.

Yes, the surgery was risky, and yes, it would weaken the leg and leave a big scar, just like the one Gabriel already had, but running up his thigh rather than down from his knee. The doctor insisted this surgery was the only way to give Gabriel a stable knee. The surgery, he added, was best done immediately. "And if he doesn't have surgery?" The doctor had a pat answer. "He could end up with arthritis by the time he's twenty." He repeated his favorite injunction: "Gabriel needs to be careful. No twisting, no jumping. And no dancing."

"How many of these quadriceps tendon surgeries do you do a year?" I inquired.

"A fair number. We did one the other day, didn't we?" the doctor replied, peering at the resident, who turned red and began to sweat profusely.

"Would it be possible to speak to that patient you just operated on?"

The resident stared at me in horror. The doctor, however, calmly replied, "That's not possible. Patient privacy, you know."

I had a sneaking suspicion this surgery hadn't gone well, and it dawned on me that at a teaching university like Michigan, it was the resident who would do the surgery, *learn to do the surgery*, on my son's knee, while the doctor supervised.

At the end of the visit, the doctor moved closer to Gabriel and squeezed his knee. A physical therapist at the clinic had told me the doctor was a hunter. At that moment, something about the ravenous way the doctor touched my son made me aware that he thought of Gabriel's leg as fresh prey. I couldn't get that image of his being a hunter out of my head. I imagined him stalking innocent animals and shooting at them. I imagined his aim was excellent. My maternal instincts told me to grab my teenage son and run out of there. And that was what I did.

WHEN GABRIEL WAS FIRST INJURED IN 1998, there was only minimal information on ACL and meniscus injuries available online. By 2003 a wealth of material could be found. Bereft of a doctor I could trust to care for Gabriel, I became an ACL information junkie. Night after night, I followed link after link: arthroscopic ACL reconstruction; ACL revision; meniscus tears; keloid revisions; septic arthritis following ACL reconstruction. I studied the surgical preferences of various knee specialists. Studying pictures of ACL surgery, I saw the bloody knees, I saw the white gook that was the cartilage.

Awake until three in the morning, I wondered what I was accomplishing other than spooking myself. I learned the names of things. I acquired a language for talking about the ACL, a part of the body I hadn't known existed until Gabriel's injury. Some thirty years ago, the medical community had decided that everyone with a loose or torn ACL should have surgery, not only athletes being paid millions for what their bodies could do. But as ACL primary surgeries became common, so did revision surgeries. Sports medicine doctors liked to boast that, with an ACL reconstruction, it was possible to return to full sports activities. What they didn't mention was that many of these surgeries failed. I entered chat rooms and discovered people preparing for their second, third, and fourth surgeries.

I compiled a list of doctors in various cities in the United States, and Gabriel agreed to go with me to see them. David understood that Gabriel and I were united by the saga of our leg injuries and that we needed to figure things out on our own. He stood back as we went in pursuit of advice. My health insurance wouldn't cover additional consultations, but I was prepared to pay any price to know everything there was to know about the knee. We met with a doctor in Los Angeles, a doctor in Cincinnati, three doctors in New York City, two more doctors in Michigan, and I spoke on the phone to a doctor in Washington and a doctor in Philadelphia. All were accomplished surgeons who worked with major athletic teams. Many were authors of popular books or specialized articles about knee surgery.

They were all amazed, and occasionally amused, that I knew so much. Some thought I was a doctor; others thought I was a nurse. None were in agreement with our doctor's plan to use a quadriceps tendon autograft. It was dangerous and would compromise the leg severely. The majority favored allografts from cadaver or donor tissue, despite the risks. Recovery was quicker and patients didn't have to sacrifice tissue from their own body; but there was a risk of transmission of AIDS and hepatitis and a possibility of serious infection, even death, if the tissue was contaminated. I cried as I read about a young man named Brian Lykins, who was twenty-four when he went in for routine knee surgery and died four days later after receiving contaminated bone tissue that had been improperly harvested from a suicide victim.

By the end of the summer we still hadn't found a doctor close to home to care for Gabriel. One day a friend suggested I find out who was the orthopedic surgeon for the Detroit Pistons, the Michigan basketball team that was my son's favorite. I got online, looked up the Pistons, and found the name of the team's public relations person. Later that day I got a message back with the name of the surgeon.

His clinic was an hour's drive from Ann Arbor, very close to Detroit. The four-lane highway was crowded with trucks and SUVs going eighty miles an hour. David drove while I held my breath. I wanted to turn around and leave when we found the clinic in a half-deserted strip mall. Inside, the carpet was old, the furniture looked scruffy. We waited for two hours in the lobby and then endured the usual half-hour wait in the examining room.

At last the doctor entered, white-haired with bushy dark eyebrows and the humble gaze of a monk. A brisk hello and then he said to Gabriel, "Why are you here?"

Gabriel replied, "I think I'm going to need surgery."

The doctor said, "What makes you think surgery is going to make things better?"

He got to work taking measurements of Gabriel's legs with a little ruler. What impressed me was that he examined both legs, not just the injured leg, as most of the doctors had done. He also studied Gabriel's hips, feet, and ankles. When he finished, he turned to me, "Questions?" His gaze was inquiring, but gentle.

I had an entire sheet of printed questions and started going down the list. He didn't rush his answers. He was the first doctor willing to acknowledge that surgery could just as likely bring on arthritis as not doing surgery. He expressed strong doubts about ACL surgery. He said he'd grown cynical because he'd seen so many failures. He'd started out doing all primary surgeries on the ACL; now it was almost all revisions. Why were they failing so much? I nearly fell off my chair when I heard him wondering aloud. No other doctor we'd met had shown this degree of self-awareness and critical thinking.

What should we do? I finally asked. Should Gabriel have surgery? The doctor sighed, looked at us with kindness. There was sadness too in his gaze.

"There's no easy answer," he replied. He couldn't assure us of anything, but he'd give it a go if we wanted.

After confronting so many overconfident doctors, it was a relief to find one wracked with doubt but trying to do the best he could. Nevertheless I still didn't want Gabriel to have surgery. Summer and fall passed. We'll wait, we'll just wait, I thought, until an answer falls from the sky. Finally it was Gabriel who said he'd lost confidence in his knee and wanted to go through with the second surgery.

But as the mid-February surgery date approached, I reached a point of high anxiety. I was crying constantly, even in Gabriel's presence.

Alone in the house a few days before the surgery, I phoned the doctor's office. His nurse responded. When I asked for more information about the doctor's experience with ACL surgeries, she grew defensive and told me that if I was unsure about his skills, maybe we should cancel the surgery. I was tempted to do just that. Instead I told her I needed to speak to the doctor one more time. She said she'd give him the message. I didn't think she would. It was Friday. The surgery was scheduled for Monday.

After dinner I sat in the kitchen reading an article about precision in ACL surgery that the doctor himself had written. The phone rang and my heart skipped a beat. It was the doctor on the line, calling back on a Friday night.

We ended up talking for two hours.

He promised to send me a German dissertation he felt offered the best research on ACL injuries.

Then he asked what kind of doctor I was. Why did I know so much about this subject? I told him I was a cultural anthropologist.

"What do people with ACL injuries do in other places, where they can't have surgery?" I asked him.

"They learn to live with their disability," he replied.

I thanked him for calling.

"I'm sorry I can't allay your fears," he said. "I really wish I could."

THE SURGERY LASTED CLOSE TO SEVEN HOURS. After it was over, the doctor came out to the waiting room and sat close to David and me. He hadn't yet eaten. He would, after he talked to us. He was still in his scrubs and smelled of soap and rubbing alcohol.

"You were right about the stretched graft," he said.

Just before Gabriel went in to surgery, I told the doctor I suspected Gabriel's ACL graft wasn't torn, but stretched out.

"I spent a long time trying to reattach it, but it wouldn't hold. I put in the allograft tissue and checked the measurements several times. Right now the operated leg has less laxity than the good leg."

"Were you able to get the graft both elastic and tight?"

He smiled. "I see you've been reading that dissertation I sent you."

I'd been worried about Gabriel's meniscus. Most of the doctors wanted to "clean it up"—in other words, remove it, which was easier than trying to sew up the tear.

"The good news," he said, "is I was able to repair Gabriel's meniscus. I didn't take any of it out. Repairing it took longer. I hope it's going to be worth it."

On that day I felt about this doctor as the poet Abba Kovner, writing in *Sloan Kettering: Poems*, felt about his doctor, "the man / whose hands have done everything for you / that a man's hands can do / and the rest is with heaven."

Afterward he prescribed doubt and uncertainty. Physical therapy? It could help. So could walking a few miles a day.

We took things slowly. Gabriel got on his crutches, started walking. In a few months he'd be graduating from high school. His teammates asked him to be the coach of their basketball team. Bravely, humbly, he returned to the same court where he was injured and coached the other kids.

He listened to the wise songs of Stevie Wonder, the blind bard with the sweet, loving voice.

On one of my trips to Cuba, when I told an acquaintance about Gabriel's knee troubles, his advice was, "Tell your son to get a girlfriend. Two or three girlfriends." I never told this to Gabriel, but he figured it out for himself. A girlfriend appeared after his surgery and provided sympathy, chocolate, and the cuddling he needed and could no longer accept from his mother.

He now had two big scars, one on the front and one on the side of his knee. It gave me a chill to see them, but I took comfort in the knowledge that my son wouldn't be sent to war. Just before he turned eighteen, the U.S. Army called to recruit him. When Gabriel said he had titanium screws in his leg, they said he wasn't eligible.

Soon after, Gabriel left home to study film in New York.

DURING THE NEXT FEW MONTHS, as I adjusted to being a mother in an empty nest, I reflected on my consuming involvement in Gabriel's knee injuries and surgeries.

I'd wanted Gabriel to be the athlete that I hadn't been because of my own leg injury as a child.

But there was also a historical substratum of anxiety that his injury had made me aware of. As a child of immigrants who'd made a quick decision to leave Cuba, and as a child immigrant myself, I knew how important it was to be able to flee at a moment's notice, to escape danger, to escape countries in revolution, countries in the midst of strife, war, suffering. How to run away if your legs won't hold you up?

It occurred to me that there's a kind of primordial power in a great chase scene, like the one Gabriel conjured in his first movie, *Run*. Perhaps the most elemental fear for all humanity is to be trapped in an unbearable situation and not be able to get away. In a chase scene we experience the need to run, at a crazy speed, to freedom.

ALL THOSE YEARS WHILE GABRIEL was growing up and becoming a man, dealing with his injuries and frightening moments of immobility, I kept running away. When I wasn't in Cuba, I was dancing tango. I ran to run away but also to reassure myself that my legs were healed and to pray that his legs would heal too.

Not long after Gabriel left home, I went to the monthly *milonga* dance party on campus. I'd been dancing for two hours and was ready to leave. Then Amesh approached.

"Would you like to dance?"

I nodded and took his hand.

He apologized before taking a step. "I'm something of a beginner. Hope you don't mind."

Amesh danced carefully. Slowly. Soulfully. He wasn't much taller than I. He had a strong chest and strong thighs. He felt solid as a tree trunk. He understood the music but was hesitant. After the first song ended, he said, "I was getting good at this a while back, but I had to have knee surgery. Now it's almost like starting from scratch."

Naturally my ears perked up. "Knee surgery? What kind?"

He replied, "ACL surgery. On both knees."

We kept dancing. We danced to four songs, sad tango songs about lost loves, lost neighborhoods, lost mothers.

When our sequence ended, we walked to the edge of the dance floor. I asked him about his knees. The first injury happened in India, when he was sixteen. But he didn't have the surgery until ten years later, when he came to the States. Then the other ACL tore during a game of golf. So he had surgery again. He was fine, though, absolutely fine. "Life goes on," he said, laughing.

"Does tango dancing bother your knees?"

"Not at all."

I told him about Gabriel, how worried I was for him, how distraught I was about his big scars.

"Your son is lucky he has someone to worry for him," Amesh said. His eyes misted a bit, and he told me he'd lost his mother when he was a child. Very young, he'd been sent away to boarding school.

Suddenly he brightened. "You want to see my scars?" Before I could speak, he rolled up his pant legs, right then and there, at the edge of the dance floor, and showed me his silky scars, one on the front of each dark-haired knee.

They were thinner, smoother, less noticeable than Gabriel's, but they were scars nonetheless.

A moment ago we had danced tango. Inhibitions had vanished. Without thinking or asking for permission, I reached down, touched the scar on his right leg, ran a finger softly along the thick rim of skin, just to see how it felt, the place where the knife had cut.

"Feels okay," I concluded.

Amesh nodded. "The doctor did a good job. It healed nicely."

We both gazed at his scars a little longer. Amesh didn't rush to cover them. He stood there, his pants rolled up to his knees, as they played "La Cumparsita," the last tango song of the evening.

a degree in hard work

....

On a sunny Tuesday around noon, Gabriel and I watch for my mother in the crowd of women emerging from her New York University office. Ten minutes later she appears.

She's wearing a striped shirt with white linen pants and fashionable white-framed sunglasses. My mother is not quite five feet tall, and she always used to wear high heels. Now that she's seventy-one and has had a knee replaced, she's in comfortable sandals. Her toenails, however, are painted bright red.

She kisses us and apologizes for being late. "Another lost diploma," she sighs, shaking her head. "Why can't students keep their diplomas in a safe place? If they're smart enough to earn a college degree, they should learn how to take care of their diplomas."

My mother got as far as high school in Cuba, but in the United States she's an expert on university diplomas. For thirty-two years she's supervised the diploma department.

"*¿A dónde vamos?*" my mother asks Gabriel. "You want Chinese? Or enchiladas, or falafel?"

Gabriel is entering his senior year as a film student at NYU, and it thrills me that he's found a place in the city that was once my home. He's learned to navigate the subway routes for the five boroughs. He has acquired an urban flair all his own and is wearing an oversized gray International Center of Photography sweatshirt that's casually matched

Mami and Gabriel in Queens,
New York, 2007. Photo by Ruth Behar.

with his old faded jeans and two-toned Adidas sneakers. His curly hair peeks out of the edges of his dark blue University of Michigan ski cap, pulled down low on his forehead. The cap is his badge of loyalty to his home state and he won't let go of it, though the maize "M" is starting to fray around the edges.

Gabriel and my mother lunch once a week.

"How about we go to the Italian place?" Gabriel suggests.

I want to weigh in on the question too. "Why don't we eat right here?" I ask, pointing to a restaurant across the street.

"What? At the Gotham?" My mother pronounces it Go-tom. *"Muy caro."* Too expensive. "When Gabrielito graduates, we'll go," she promises.

Ever since Gabriel entered NYU, my mother's big dream has been to bestow his diploma upon him when he graduates.

"We're wasting time," Gabriel points out. "Let's go to the Italian place."

"Sí, vamos," my mother says.

We walk half a block to a restaurant with slinky multicolored halogen lights. The waiter seats us at a quiet table in the back, and we each order the lunch special: a mixed salad and pizza for $8.50.

As the pizzas arrive, my mother pulls out a sheet of paper folded in half. She passes it to me. "Can you look at this and see if my English is okay?"

In the loopy handwriting of a teenage girl, my mother states that she plans to retire in August. Gabriel reads the letter. "So this is it? You're really going to retire?"

"Yeah, this time I'm going to do it."

For six years, ever since she turned sixty-five, my mother has been threatening to call it quits. My father retired nine years ago at the age of sixty-four, unable to tolerate even one more day as a traveling textile salesman. But my mother keeps deferring her retirement date. She can't bear to leave. More than once she's told me about women who retire and die soon after.

Tears spring to my mother's eyes when she says to Gabriel, "I don't want to retire yet. But I feel I should. Your grandfather is alone in the house, and I'm tired of waking up at six in the morning and taking the subway from Queens. But I get to the office and everyone says, 'You look so cute,' and I feel good."

I point to the retirement letter. "Mami, aren't you going to write a more personal letter to everyone at the office?"

"Look inside," she says. Folded inside the paper is the letter from her heart: "I feel like I am leaving parts of my family."

As I correct my mother's letter, I think about how both our lives changed course in 1974, the year the feminist movement broke into our immigrant household. That autumn I left home to go to college, and my mother took a job as a secretary at the university.

Her hope was to supplement Papi's salary. What she didn't anticipate was that she'd find a second home in an office filled with Latinas like herself, who spoke Spanish but who were eager to be part of American life. Mami discovered she took pride in receiving a paycheck, providing health insurance for my father, and learning new skills.

She enjoyed socializing with her colleagues, celebrating their birthdays with her delicious Cuban bread pudding made with rum and lots of raisins.

Dabbing her eyes with a tissue, my mother asks Gabriel if he minds that she won't be the one to give him his diploma.

"It's okay, Nana," he assures her.

I return the corrected retirement letter to my mother, and she stuffs it into her handbag without looking at it.

She glances at her watch. "I have to get back to work."

Gabriel and I hurry to keep up with her. As I watch her vanish into her building through the revolving doors, I half hope she'll hold on long enough to be able to say to her grandson, "Here's your diploma. Keep it somewhere safe."

A few days later, Mami calls on the phone. "I'm going to wait another month to retire," she announces. "But only one more month." She pauses. "After that, I leave, for sure."

la silla

....

When we left Cuba, we settled on a street in Queens that was lined with rows of six-story red brick buildings. Chain-link fences surrounded the patches of green lawn in front of each building. Jabbed into the dirt were signs that read "Keep Off the Grass." Those may have been some of the first words I learned in English.

The sea-drenched streets of La Habana, shaded by frangipani and royal palms, were far away; so too the bright lights and skyscrapers of Manhattan that my mother had dreamed of. Mami thought those brick buildings in Queens were ugly, but she didn't dare say that aloud. We'd followed in the path of her older sister, Sylvia, whom Mami looked up to. Just before the Revolution began in Cuba, my Aunt Sylvia married my Uncle Bill, an *americano*, and moved into one of those brick buildings.

Only years later did Mami admit how disappointed she was to discover that this was the America where we'd landed. What mattered was to reunite our family. My parents and Mori and I lived in an apartment on the sixth floor. Sylvia and Bill and my cousins, Danny and Linda, lived on the fourth floor. Baba and Zayde lived on the third floor with my Uncle Miguel, then in his late teens. We children roamed in and out of the three apartments freely, as if no doors separated them.

I was the oldest of the four children, three years older than Mori and Linda, and two years older than Danny. I was the first to go to school.

Because I was so miserable—suddenly finding myself unable to speak to my classmates because I didn't know English—I insisted we play school after I returned home. Re-creating my school day in the world of make-believe, I could be in charge rather than being a loser. As the only one who knew anything about school, I insisted on being the teacher; Mori, Linda, and Danny were the students.

By the age of six, in first grade, I felt very grown up. As an immigrant child, I'd lost interest, or possibly faith, in dolls, but I begged my parents to buy me a blackboard. Papi wasn't keen on the idea, but Mami advocated on my behalf, and they got me a blackboard that teetered on rickety wooden legs. It came with a drawer for storing the chalk and eraser. Just like my real teacher, I had an envelope with gold stars. I'd paste them on the "assignments" of my "students" if they did well and behaved in class.

Linda received all the stars. She was obedient. Mori daydreamed. Danny never sat still. Eventually the two boys formed an alliance and wrecked my classroom, becoming hopelessly unruly. No amount of threats that they'd never earn a gold star brought them into line.

What painful recognition I feel gazing at pictures of myself then—an uncertain smile, hair uncombed. I wore knee-high socks that sagged, black-and-white loafers a size too big. I had a plaid skirt with a lumpy hem. Mami rolled it up and sewed it with loose stitches, so she could let it down as I grew taller. For some mysterious reason, I liked to button my blouses all the way up to the top, primly, so they pinched my neck. I looked the part of the frumpy schoolteacher.

So why does it come as a surprise to me that I did eventually become a schoolteacher? It is my teaching that supports my travels, and when I'm not on the road, I'm standing in front of the room lecturing to students. But the truth is I'd prefer to sit in the corner and not have to speak. I'm more a listener than a talker. And I don't forget my humble roots as a shy immigrant child who spent a year in the dumb class.

I had a high school teacher, Mrs. Rodríguez, who told me I was smart and should go away to college. A Cuban immigrant, she'd taught literature at the University of Havana, but when she came to New York her degree was worthless. To make ends meet, she became a Spanish teacher at Forest Hills High School, slowly accruing the credits for her Ph.D. in literature in night courses at NYU. She introduced me to the novels of Gabriel García Márquez and the short stories of Jorge Luis Borges and inspired me to write poems in Spanish. As Mrs. Rodríguez's favorite student, I was invited out each week for a kitchen sink ice cream sundae at Jahn's on Queens Boulevard. I loved hearing Mrs. Rodríguez speak her melodious Spanish. She sang when she talked, and she bared her heart to me during these outings but never let me forget *she* was the teacher. With a gentle wink of her blue eyes, she'd correct me if I failed to address her in the formal *usted*.

I kept it a secret from Mami and Papi that I spent so much time after school with Mrs. Rodríguez. It upset Papi that she was giving me advice about my future. He didn't want me to go to college. He believed that a good girl stayed in her father's house until a man came along and married her.

Mami understood me. She sneaked money out of the checkbook so I could pay the college application fees.

Once the acceptances arrived, with scholarship offers to boot, I expected Papi to change his mind and be happy. Instead he was furious. I shed many tears over dinners of *arroz con pollo* during my last few months of high school, failing to convince him it was important for me to get an education. My mother shed many more tears in the bedroom with my father, who admonished her for giving in to my wishes. Late at night, sleeping with my ear pressed against the wall of the bedroom I shared with Mori, which adjoined theirs, I heard Mami's cries.

Finally Papi relented and let me go. But there was rage in his surrender. And maybe also love, though I couldn't understand that back then. Love for a daughter who was leaving home. I set off for Wesleyan University, just a few hours away in Middletown, Connecticut, filled with feelings of doom. Even with a scholarship, college was expensive, and Mami let me know in our weekly phone calls that my studies were proving to be a financial strain on them. Two months into college, I met with the dean and figured out a plan to take summer tutorials so I could graduate a year early. After finishing college in three years (including spending a semester abroad in Spain), I went straight to graduate school, supported this time by a full scholarship. At twenty-six, I earned my Ph.D.

Mrs. Rodríguez said I was smart, but I never believed it. I feared I needed to stay in school in order not to grow dumb. But in school, to this very day, I often feel so dumb! Attending a symposium recently with faculty and graduate students at my university, I felt pathetically tongue-tied, unable to think of anything smart to say.

But now my colleagues, demonstrating huge kindness and generosity, have nominated me for a collegiate professorship, a named chair.

Rather than run out and shout the news to everyone in sight, I keep it to myself. I am not at all sure I deserve such an honor.

I don't tell even Mami and Papi.

Months pass and finally, at the airport, returning from an academic event in Atlanta, and with a little time to kill, I decide to give Mami and Papi a call in New York.

Mami, as always, answers the phone.

"*Me van a dar una silla. Lo llaman así—un* chair."

"*¿Y Ruti, te van a pagar más? ¿Te suben el sueldo?*"

"*Un poco.*"

Mami doesn't think I earn enough money. When I started teaching and Mami asked about my salary, she lamented, "*¿Por eso te estas quemando la vista?*" For that you're burning out your eyes?

"*¡Alberto!*" she calls to my father, who is down in the basement.

Papi is watching a football game. He hates to be interrupted but picks up the phone.

"Hello, Ruth."

He calls me Ruth lately, not Ruti, my childhood name. I wonder whether he does it to emphasize the distance between us, the unforgiveable mutiny I enacted when I left home over thirty years ago. But maybe he's just acknowledging, finally, that I'm no longer his little girl.

"I just wanted to tell you—they're giving me a chair."

"*¿Que es eso—un* chair? *No entiendo.*"

I try to think of how to explain it to him, stumbling so much I stutter. "*Es algo muy importante.* It's the highest honor they give professors at our university."

"And they call it like that—*una silla*?"

"That means it's permanent. They want me at the university forever."

"Okay. Talk more to your mother."

He clicks off. No words of praise. No words of congratulations.

I know Papi never forgave Abuelo for forcing him to give up his dream of studying to become an architect. With his gorgeous penmanship, Papi would have designed the most beautiful houses. But Abuelo demanded he help him peddle blankets door to door, so Papi ended up studying accounting, the only subject offered during evening classes in the 1950s at the University of Havana. Coming to the United States soon after, and having to start life over as a penniless immigrant, he worked seven days a week to support my mother, my brother, and me, working at a desk job from Monday to Friday and fumigating apartments in Spanish Harlem on weekends. Eventually he moved up, becoming a traveling textile salesman, selling the *shmates*, as he often put it, that nobody in the United States wanted to buy to merchants in Latin America.

Perhaps Papi resents my education? Perhaps he thinks it's a pity so much precious knowledge has been wasted on a woman? Perhaps I've never shown sufficient appreciation for the sacrifices he made for me as a father? I can only speculate about what he thinks, what thorns are scratching at his heart. Such a long time being his daughter, and I still can't read my father's silences.

Hearing the gate agent announce over the loudspeaker that the first-class passengers can board the plane, I leap to my feet, glad to line up with the other privileged travelers. On domestic flights I'm sometimes upgraded to first class, my reward for traveling so much. Between the plush seating and getting plenty of water to drink on the flight, I'll get schoolwork done. There's always more schoolwork to be done when you're a teacher.

As the plane rises into the sky, I pull out my red pen and the writing assignments of my students. I see ways they can improve, ways they can say what they want to say more clearly, more forcefully. I figure the plane can't possibly crash so long as the students are awaiting my response to their work.

I concentrate well when my head is in the clouds. I scribble dozens of comments on the margins of the papers. I remember to say something positive to each student. Everyone gets a gold star—for effort, if nothing else.

As we touch down, it dawns on me that what Papi wants is a gold star—from me. And as old as I am, a middle-aged woman now, I'm still waiting for a gold star—from Papi.

part two

THE KINDNESS OF STRANGERS

from those who don't forget you

....

I'd gone to college intending to be a poet and a fiction writer. In my last year, undergoing a change of heart, I switched to anthropology and applied to graduate school. I had a lot of doubts about whether I'd made the right decision. I knew I was accepted at Princeton because I'd made a good impression on James Fernandez, the professor who was to become my mentor. After many years of carrying out research in West Africa, Jim had begun new fieldwork in Asturias, where his grandfather was from. He'd received a grant to take graduate students to do anthropological fieldwork in a few provinces of northern Spain and was scouting for willing candidates. Jim lined up Joseba Zulaika to go to the Basque Country and John Holmquist to go to Santander. He needed a student to work in León, in Santa María del Monte, a tiny village (population 120). Did I want to go? Sure, I said, with no idea what I was getting myself into. It was 1978 and I was twenty-one.

As the June departure date loomed closer, I despaired at the thought of going alone to Spain. In the throes of youthful love, I wanted David, who was my boyfriend then, to come with me. I'd completed my undergraduate degree at Wesleyan University and finished my first year of graduate school at Princeton while David was in his last year at Wesleyan, where I would have been had I not finished in three years. To continue to be separated for the whole summer felt unbearable. And I was eager to show David around Spain. I'd been to Madrid on a semester abroad program and spent a summer in Catalunya. I wanted David to know this place that I considered part of my heritage as a Cuban immigrant and a descendant of Spanish Jews. At that time, David was a student of Russian and mathematics, but I knew he'd help in every way he could with my fieldwork.

I was nervous about asking Jim to let David accompany me and waited until the last possible moment to speak to him. His immediate response was that David would be a distraction from my research. He insisted I go to Spain on my own. "What's three months?" he said. "You'll be back before you know it." I'm not sure how I got up the nerve, but I told Jim I wouldn't go unless David went with me. Jim held firm and said he'd have to rescind his offer. Finally, David wrote a detailed letter expressing his sincere interest in learning about Spain and fieldwork methods. Jim relented but said we could both go only if we told people in the village that we were married. He warned us that social values there were very conservative. It was just three years after the death of General Franco. We'd shock and offend everyone in Santa María if they knew we were unmarried and living together—living in sin.

I was prepared to tell this lie without guilt. David and I were almost married. But the burden of that lie was augmented by a second lie, and that made it heavier to carry. I'd decided to keep it a secret from my parents that I was going to Spain with David. That David wasn't Jewish, that I'd chosen a man from outside our tribe as my boyfriend, had caused them immense sadness and grief. Papi declared me dead. He didn't perform mourning rituals and forsake me completely, as is customary among Orthodox Jews, but he stopped speaking to me. Mami talked to me only to tell me how much they were suffering.

I'd been cast out. I was no longer welcome at home.

I held my breath as I called to say goodbye. Mami said she was glad I was going to Spain on my own. "Is David still your boyfriend?" she asked. I said no. I could feel the relief in her voice as she said, "I'll tell your father."

I took a bus to JFK and found David waiting anxiously in a corner of the airport. Falling into his arms, embracing him with desperation, I wept like an orphan.

In Madrid we found a cheap hotel near the Atocha railway station. We took the train to León the next day. Unable to afford a taxi, we dragged our suitcases down the avenues and cobblestoned streets until we reached the oldest plaza in León, where we were meeting Jim and his wife, Renate, for lunch before heading to Santa María.

Back then, I found Jim intimidating. Tall and limber from mountain climbing, he was white-haired and spoke in a whisper. I had to get very close to hear him. Renate, similarly white-haired, had translucent blue eyes that wanted to peer into your soul. We sat across the table from each other eating a hearty *cocido* of chick peas, beef, and sausage that made me break out in a sweat. I was certain Jim and Renate were gazing at me disapprovingly for lacking the strength of will to carry out my first fieldwork alone.

The sun was still bright as we drove to the village in their rental car. I'd brought an enormous suitcase filled with more clothes and shoes than I needed. Jim was appalled by its size and squeezed it into the backseat between David and me. Unable to glance at David for reassurance, I stared out the window at the adobe houses and soft meadows. The palette of the countryside was changing from brown and yellow to resplendent green. Stunning long tresses hung heavily from the old willow trees. We wound around a long curve, and then Jim made a sudden left and turned up the road.

Santa María, the place Jim had chosen for my field site, came into view. He'd made housing arrangements with the schoolteacher, who lived at the entrance to the village. After knocking on the door for a while, we realized she wasn't home. A man named José Antonio, who was fixing a drainage pipe next to her house while his young son Francisco watched, told us that on Sundays the schoolteacher went with her husband to his hometown of Boñar. Jim explained our situation. José Antonio listened sympathetically but had no idea what arrangements had been made. He offered to put us up in the home of his parents. We could stay for the night. On Monday the schoolteacher would return and we could speak to her.

A moment later, David and I were picking up our suitcases and preparing to spend the night at the home of strangers, who also hadn't been expecting two young guests to appear out of nowhere.

There's a picture that Jim took of me, that I've since lost, but I remember it vividly. I was wearing a white blouse, rolled up to the elbows, and a long brown skirt with ruffles at the hem. And tall boots with laces that crisscrossed in front. My hair was tied up in a knot at the top of my head. I rarely wore it loose then. I looked like a woman from the pioneer days of the American frontier. Jim snapped the picture as I tried to wedge my way through the huge wooden door while lifting my abominably heavy suitcase. That's the first image I have of myself as an anthropologist: in that long skirt, lugging that suitcase I could barely squeeze through the door.

When I stepped out again, Jim whispered, "Good luck," and he and Renate sped off, hoping to cross the Cantabrian Mountains before nightfall.

I didn't have a chance to ask him, Now what do I do?

María, the mother of José Antonio, showed us upstairs to the bedroom where David and I would sleep. She ordered her husband, Virgilio, who was older and smaller than she and had a limp, to wait in the kitchen, so he wouldn't tire himself. Even though she wasn't cooking, she wore an apron over her dress.

A mischievous sparkle lit up her dark eyes. "Have you been married long?" she asked. She spoke to me, because I was the one who knew Spanish.

I scrambled for an answer. "A year," I replied. I could feel the cheap silver ring on my finger digging into my flesh. I wasn't used to it yet. David was wearing a ring as well. We'd bought them at the last minute before leaving Princeton.

"Really? And you both look so young. Like brother and sister."

The sun had gone down and there was a sudden chill in the air. María noticed me squeezing my arms against my chest to keep warm and pulled out an extra blanket from the armoire and set it down on the bed.

"I don't think you two are murderers. You're not going to kill us, are you? And we're not going to kill you."

With those words, she left us alone to spend our first night in Santa María, clinging to each other because the chill grew worse in the wee hours. It was June, I thought, June and very cold. Then I remembered we were at the foot of the mountains.

The next morning I spoke to the schoolteacher and learned that she'd arranged for us to stay with María's brother-in-law, Balbino, the younger brother of Virgilio, and his wife, Hilaria, only a few houses away. How was it possible that María didn't know this? Later I would learn that the two families had quarreled years earlier about an inheritance and ever since had kept their distance. María waved goodbye reluctantly, evidently sorry to see us go. She very graciously didn't charge us for the night we spent at her home, where we'd been good enough not to murder her and her husband. She was certain we were rich and that Balbino would be the one to profit from the rent we'd pay him. It wouldn't be long before María and everyone else in the village learned David and I were just a pair of poor students with little to offer other than our desire to learn what made their lives meaningful.

ANOTHER ENORMOUS OLD WOODEN DOOR led into Balbino and Hilaria's house. I now understood why they needed such doors—so cows, sheep, donkeys, and other farm animals could come and go.

María and Virgilio were retired and kept only a few chickens and rabbits in cages. That was why their house felt ghostly. But upon entering the home of Balbino and Hilaria, I saw animals roaming about freely and relaxing in stables that encircled the courtyard. As in a fairy tale, the animals were treated like characters with human personalities. The cows had the most beautiful names. I'll always remember La Linda and La Mariposa, whose faces shone with infinite patience. They were the same velvety brown color of the mud that had been used to make the adobe walls of the houses, before people switched to industrial red brick.

Until that moment, I'd never been inside a house where human beings shared their living space with farm animals. No one in my family had even kept cats or dogs. Unlike some other children in Queens, whose parents sent them away to summer camp so they could get a taste of the countryside, I stayed home. Not that my parents could have afforded to send me to camp. The truth is, I wouldn't have wanted to go. As a little girl in Cuba, I'd been taught to be ladylike and keep my dresses clean and pretty, and growing up in gritty New York, I'd held on to that prissiness as best I could. I felt no desire to be in the countryside, where I'd be forced to live in a wooden cabin and sit around a burning fire singing silly songs and getting all dirty and mosquito-bitten.

Having shunned the countryside and lived a totally urban existence, I now found myself walking through a small side door to the part of the house where Hilaria and Balbino lived. That they were both still engaged in farm work was evident from their sunburned skin and roughened hands.

"Let me show you the upstairs," Hilaria said briskly and in a voice so loud she could be heard in the next village. Over time I'd learn that Hilaria always spoke as if she were addressing an auditorium full of people. Hers was a voice used to hailing cows and sheep that wandered.

She led the way. David and I followed her past the bedroom she shared with Balbino. It had a narrow balcony looking onto the street. In a far corner of the house, where the floors slanted, was the bedroom we'd occupy for the next three months. Unlike the bedroom in María's house, this bedroom was warm and cozy. I was delighted I wouldn't have to sleep in the cold.

"*Qué calentito, qué bueno,*" I said.

Hilaria smiled. She adjusted the kerchief that was wrapped around her head. Then I noticed the smell, a distinct odor, I wasn't sure of what, an odor of sopping wet grass after the rain, rotting flowers, a hint of sweetness turned bitter and nauseating.

"What's the smell?" I asked.

"The pigs," Hilaria said. "They live below you."

MY FIRST FIELDNOTES SHOULD HAVE mentioned the pigs. Curiously, I never wrote about them, though for three months they were such an important olfactory presence in our lives. I also didn't write about the crucifix above our bed, which made me uncomfortable. I took it down before we went to sleep. The next morning I put it back up. I'd continue to perform this secretive ritual for the length of our stay in Santa María. An instinct of fear and self-preservation had led me to decide not to reveal to the village people that I was Jewish. If it would shock them to know I was living in sin with a man, I figured they'd be more deeply shocked to discover I was a descendant of the expelled Jews of Spain. At the time of the Inquisition, Jews who pretended to convert to Catholicism were taunted as *marranos*, another word for pigs. Now I was a *marrana*, a hidden Jew living upstairs from the pigs.

Instead of the pigs, it was a baby lamb I felt inspired to write about, a lamb in distress. I had grown up speaking Spanish at home with my Cuban family, but I didn't know the word for baby lamb. It was in Santa María that I learned it was called by the tender name of *corderín*.

The word and the lamb made an impression on me. On Monday, June 5, 1978, I recorded on my manual typewriter, "The corderín at last is quiet. Now at 10:00 at night, its mother returns finally to give it milk to suck; for two hours it has let out an eerie cry of hunger and desire, the hunger for nurture, the desire for the warm breast. As the peace settles around the yard, darkness slowly comes, and the cold. Every few moments now it is the mother's full baritone we hear; not a word anymore from the child."

My natural inclination, before I had any idea what fieldnotes were supposed to look like, was to try to write poetically. After all, I'd once had literary aspirations. Gradually I'd learn to stifle the poetry in everything I saw around me, growing deaf to the nightly cries of the baby lamb as I sought to acquire the authoritative voice of the anthropologist who relentlessly seeks information and nothing else. This is what disappoints me when I reread my later fieldnotes. The notes I kept in the summer of 1978 were full of the sense of enchantment, as if I'd fallen from the sky into a place unlike any other. But afterward, when I returned to Santa María in the summer of 1979, and during the long stretch I spent there from the summer of 1980 until the fall of 1981, I wrote exclusively about land tenure, inheritance, and the historical documents I read about the village and the region, only what was relevant to my dissertation.

Now I wish I'd written more about baby lambs and the intense smells in the village—the odors of piss and shit from the animals, the scent of heather in the fields.

Following my first summer in Santa María, when I returned to Princeton, I was asked to write a report about my fieldwork. Several professors in the department found the report so abysmal that at a faculty meeting they discussed terminating my short season in graduate school. My work lacked academic rigor. I didn't understand theoretical concepts. They expressed the concern that I wasn't malleable—

"unteachable" is the term I recall being used. They were right: I resisted being schooled, resisted being "disciplined." I wanted to become an anthropologist, but I refused to surrender to the dry analytical language I was being taught in graduate school. Still, I didn't want to flunk out. I lacked the courage to return to New York and work a day job as a secretary and try to write my poems and my novel on the weekends.

I was going to stick to anthropology even if it killed me.

At the time, too young, too powerless, I didn't realize I'd have to reshape anthropology precisely so it wouldn't kill me, so it wouldn't kill my soul.

First I had to survive graduate school.

Jim believed in my intellectual abilities and persuaded his colleagues to give me a second chance. Afterward, not to disappoint him, I became rigorous, focused, adept at spouting theoretical concepts. I permitted myself to be teachable and got promoted from the dumb class to the head of the class. Jim never again had to come to my rescue.

I defended my dissertation so successfully that the committee recommended it be published immediately. Afterward, when we had a moment alone, Jim told me, in one of his whispers, that he'd expected something different from me. "Different?" I asked. "How so?" He paused. He wanted to be careful with his words. Finally he said he thought there'd be more poetry, more stories. What had happened? I detected sorrow in his voice, though we were celebrating my achievement.

I didn't know how to answer him.

THE SECOND ENTRY IN MY EARLIEST fieldnotes concerned the making of a table so I could write. On Tuesday, June 6, 1978, I reflected on the labor that had gone into this project: "At 1:00 this afternoon, upon returning from a walk . . . I find Balbino and Hilaria busy thinking about how to make a table for me. This morning I told Hilaria that

I needed a desk of some sort for my typewriter; a block of wood and two legs, I said, would be enough. She told Balbino this." I gave an account of the different scraps of lumber that Balbino considered using to fashion a desk for me. "We measured off 95 centimeters 'para cada cara' [for each side] and then Balbino went and fetched a chain saw. He sawed off the two faces and turned and smiled at me. He set the two slabs on the wooden frame and asked me to position them correctly—'asientalos.' This I did, and then he went off to get a hammer and nails." Hilaria scrubbed the base and legs, left over from an old table, and then wiped the desktop that Balbino had made. We brought the desk upstairs and discovered it stood lopsided on the sloping floor. "Balbino brought back a few small pieces of wood. He set one underneath the short leg and the table ceased to wiggle. I put my typewriter on it. Here I am, with the sturdiest table I could want, made to order."

I was touched by the kindness of Balbino and Hilaria and the trouble they took to create a desk for me from the scraps of lumber they had in their house. While I might have written my notes on their kitchen table, I'd requested a desk so as not to disturb them, but also so I could write in the privacy of my bedroom. (During the day it didn't smell that bad.) With a laptop computer it's possible to write anywhere, on any surface, but not so with a manual typewriter, which demands that you pound out the letters forcefully, one by one. My first fieldnotes were written on that desk. It didn't sag or buckle. It held up all summer.

I'd been warned to make a carbon copy of all my notes and send them home for safekeeping. Horror stories abounded of anthropologists losing their fieldnotes in a mislaid suitcase or a sudden fire or other natural disaster. When I typed my notes, I inserted a piece of carbon paper between two sheets of loose leaf paper so I could keep the original and mail the copy to my mother in New York. Since David was with me secretly, I never mentioned him in the notes, which felt strange, since we were inseparable, but I couldn't blow my cover.

Mami read all my notes. Though we were estranged, she wanted to know how I was doing. (Papi was still too upset with me to want to know.) It was a time before the Internet, before email, before cell phones. There wasn't a single telephone in the village. Our only way of staying in touch was through regular postal mail, which took two weeks in each direction. Telegrams we hoped never to have to send, since they were for the delivery of bad news. I imagine my fieldnotes gave my mother another window on my life—on what I was seeing and learning. She was the audience for my notes and also the keeper of my notes, saving them until I reclaimed them, which I did only recently.

But Mami would have had to read the notes with a microscope to find me. I didn't write about myself. I hid behind the notes. I became a sounding board for people in Santa María, who wanted to express the troubling inferiority they felt at a time when the world was modernizing and globalizing and they were being left behind. "How had we found the village?" they wanted to know. "Why had we come to their village, of all the places we could have gone?" I always told the story about El Profesor and La Señora, who noticed the village from the highway and saw its landscape turn from burnt red to bright green as streams of water slowly soaked the dry fields and made them lush, all thanks to the *pantano*, the dam and irrigation system the villagers had built by themselves. "Ah, yes," people responded with satisfaction, "yes, we did build it ourselves." Then I'd say that El Profesor thought that such a place, where people had come together on their own to improve things for themselves, was well worth the attention of a young anthropology student.

They knew David and I had come from far away. We were often asked, "Is it winter over there in America now?" They'd heard of people who'd journeyed across the sea to Buenos Aires, where the seasons were backward, and they assumed we inhabited the same America.

They couldn't comprehend our need to stay for such a long time. The idea of tourism was that people traveled from one country to another to see things of value and beauty. Why had El Profesor chosen a miserable place, *un lugar tan mísere*? I was told, *"Aquí no hay nada que ver, aquí solo hay trabajo."* (Here there's nothing to see, here there's only work to do.) A woman remarked that since I'd come to Santa María, I should work as they did: *escabar, segar, regar* (hoe, reap, irrigate). Overhearing this, another woman said, *"Como nosotros no debe trabajar, como burras, como esclavos, hasta que nos morimos."* (She shouldn't work like we do, like donkeys, like slaves, until we die.) Hilaria said the work they did was "brutal" and that they worked like "brutes."

David and I had arrived just after the height of the rural exodus, when vast numbers of people broke their ties to the countryside and migrated to cities in Spain and Europe. And we'd arrived just before mechanization crushed the small farmers who lived in villages and made a living from their *cuatro vacas and cuatro tierras* (four cows and four fields).

Balbino and Hilaria, in their mid-fifties, were working their own plots of land with a pair of cows yoked together, as were several other families who'd stayed, and they were milking the cows and raising sheep and chickens and rabbits and pigs for their own sustenance and also to sell. They grew vegetables and fruit that they ate all year round. That first summer one of the most surprising things I was given to eat was a withered gray apple that had been stored in their cellar for a year. When I hesitated to bite into it, Balbino grew angry. "It's still good. It doesn't look like a pretty red apple from the store, but it's still good."

In today's language we'd say that Balbino and Hilaria and their neighbors were pursuing a sustainable way of life, eating locally and leaving a modest carbon footprint, but they saw themselves as a backward people, clinging helplessly to their dignity. What consoled them was that they knew they were among the precious few left in the world who could wrest food from the earth. As one man put it, *"Llegará un día en que tengamos que comer hierro."* (A day will come when we will have to eat iron.)

Even as they accepted urbanization as inevitable, they were disenchanted by their own failed efforts to embrace it. In Santa María they prided themselves on their tradition of solving problems as a community. They'd been the first village in the area to have running water. But in their ignorance, they'd built only one canal for one pipe, for clean water. At first, this arrangement seemed fine. But when bathrooms were added, people discovered they needed another pipe, for dirty water; otherwise all the filth collected in the street.

As Hilaria showed us their bathroom, she said we could wash up in the sink each day and take baths in the tub on Sundays, as they did, before going to Mass. The toilet, she said, was to be used only for *las aguas menores* (the smaller waters).

To be sure we understood, she led us out to the *corral*, their larger stable, where La Linda and La Mariposa made their home with three other cows whose names I've sadly forgotten. She pointed to a pile of hay and a heap of manure. Over there, that was where you did the other thing.

I looked perplexed.

Hilaria gave the explanation for dummies: You made a nest for yourself with the hay, squatted, and when you finished you mixed the hay and your shit together, then with the pitchfork you tossed it into the heap.

I tried not to look shocked by the notion of spending intimate moments with La Linda and La Mariposa. I remembered that some of my fellow graduate students, who worked in New Guinea and Africa, said Spain was "too comfortable a place" to do anthropology. How wrong they were, I thought, as I steeled my intestines for a summer of constipation.

Week after week, Balbino had to load all the accumulated shit into their wooden cart, yoke together La Linda and La Mariposa to transport it, and deposit the stinking gook in the fields. No task was more

lowly: piling loads of shit into the cart one shovelful at a time and un-
loading it in the fields, then arranging the shit in tidy piles so it could
bake in the sun and become compost.

For people in Santa María this wasn't the only brutal form of work
they did. They cut hay by hand with a scythe. They plowed the rocky
terrain with their yoked pair of cows. They picked potatoes until their
kidneys ached and their hands bled. They irrigated their fields, breaking up clumps of soil with their hoes and getting so wet that afterward
their bones felt like mush. They harvested wheat and rye mostly by
hand, the chaff forming a cloud over their heads and the dust getting
into their eyes and throats and noses and every pore of their skin. They
slaughtered their own pigs, chickens, rabbits, and sheep and made sau-
sages and stews. They produced butter from the milk of their cows and
soap from the fat of their sheep. They roasted peppers grown in their
kitchen gardens and canned them. They boiled the tomatoes they'd
harvested and made sauce. They concocted jams from their plums.
They braided garlic and onions. And they carefully laid down each
year's harvest of apples and potatoes in a cool, dark cellar so they'd have
them to eat for twelve months until the next harvest. The shepherds
drove their sheep into the hills, but each neighbor had to take a turn
taking all the cows in the village to pasture every day. They lived ninety
kilometers from the Cantabrian Sea, yet only a handful of villagers had
ever seen it. Vacations were impossible, even in the winter; the animals
couldn't be left unattended or they'd die. But on Sundays everyone
rested. Balbino said, "If we don't rest from our work for at least a day,
then what are we? Just *burros.*"

La tierra es muy señorita was an expression I heard frequently. The
land was a young lady, a princess, and she required absolute dedica-
tion, even servitude. Yet, despite all that backbreaking work to sustain
themselves, people relied more and more on the goods that came from
outside the village. Vendors pulled up in vans throughout the week,

selling everything imaginable. The *fresquero* sold oranges and bananas and other fresh fruits the villagers didn't grow. The *panadero* sold the round *hogazas* of bread because the women no longer baked their own. The *ultramarinos* man sold canned anchovies, bags of almonds, enormous bottles of olives. The wine man sold cheap red wine and bottles of *gaseosa* with which to dilute it and make it sparkly. Someone else sold detergent. A truck came every other week with the *bombonas*, the orange tanks full of natural gas that were used for heating water and the stoves.

The children and grandchildren of the villagers, living in León, Madrid, and Bilbao, came back on weekends and in the summertime, pulling up in their new cars and sporting fashionable jeans and T-shirts. With money in their pockets, they tried to convince the elders that for Spain to progress, it was necessary to spend, spend, spend rather than save, save, save, as they'd been accustomed to doing all their lives, hiding their money under the mattress. *"Tiene que correr el dinero,"* the elders were told. Money had to flow. New ideas had to be allowed to flow too. The people who'd remained in Santa María and other villages throughout Spain were to blame for the country's backwardness. They were barring the way to progress. The new urban dwellers aspired to have *un piso, un coche, y un chalet* (a city apartment, a car, and a vacation home in the countryside). They shook their heads, condemning those who chose to work brutishly in the country: *"No están preparados para la democracia."* (They aren't ready for democracy.)

Most everyone in Santa María believed in self-reliance. As Balbino put it, *"Esto es lo más pobre de todo España. Aquí cada uno es su propio dueño. Aquí uno tendrá dos vacas y otro tres y otro cuatro, pero más o menos cada uno tiene lo suyo."* (This is the poorest region of Spain. Here everyone is his own boss. Here you might have two cows, and someone else has three or four, but more or less everyone has something of his own.)

When I spent a full year there for my dissertation research, I was told I should raise my own chickens so I wouldn't have to buy eggs. Everyone had known hunger. Balbino ranted about how people had gotten too spoiled. In the past, he said, you lived on what you grew on your land, and you killed an underfed pig and made *chorizo* and *jamón* that had to last for an entire year. But even those who rarely left the village had by then gotten televisions, and they had seen all that was out there, in the world, to desire. They developed a longing for numerous things they couldn't produce themselves. These wants were regarded as *vicios*, as vices. People understood that, once you started wanting, there was no end. So they tried not to want so much. For breakfast they continued to cook their *sopas de ajo*, garlic soup topped with bread rinds, on their wood-burning stoves. They'd acquired gas stoves, since it was what you were supposed to have, but they hated them because they cooked too fast and burned the food and burned their money. They had freshly tiled bathrooms with bright shining mirrors and glistening porcelain sinks, but shitting took place in the stables with the cows.

My sympathies were entirely with the people of Santa María. I had no solutions for the terrible contradictions they were facing. I felt for them, felt the struggle they waged to hold onto their old way of life while succumbing to the temptations of consumerism. And they, in turn, took me in with a generosity I didn't feel I deserved, for I was a liar withholding truths from them and even from my own parents. But I'd stroked their vanity, told them their greatest treasure was their living history—their legends and folklore and old village documents and that they remembered the ancient ways of working the land—and consequently they treated me like a lost grandchild who'd traveled from afar to validate their choice, to assure them they weren't crazy to stay on the land.

At the time I was reading Raymond Williams's *The Country and the City* and took his pro-agrarian message to heart: "If we are to survive at all, we shall have to develop and extend our working agricultures. . . .

Work on the land will have to become more rather than less important and central. It is one of the most striking deformations of industrial capitalism that one of our most central and urgent and necessary activities should have been so displaced, in space or in time or in both, that it can be plausibly associated only with the past or with distant lands." Although I believed these words, I recognized I was the most unlikely spokesperson for any campaign to return to the land.

Earnest as I was as a young woman, I was useless as a helper in the fields. I have intense allergies to trees, pollen, and ragweed. Upon arriving in Santa María, I broke out in hives. My sneezing fits left me breathless. My eyes were always teary, as if I'd just watched a sad movie. A doctor came twice a week to the village to check the blood pressure of the elders. I was a regular patient too, getting allergy shots to control my body's fierce reaction to the vegetation bursting into bloom everywhere. But the shots weren't strong enough to alleviate my symptoms. I'd continually scratch my itchy skin or blow my nose as I pitched hay into the cart or pulled out weeds. As if that weren't bad enough, I lacked the stamina to witness the routine slaughters that sustain life in the countryside. Seeing the proverbial headless chicken running through the yard after being hacked with a knife, or watching as a rabbit's days came to an end by having one of its eyes smashed and the other pop out and roll to the floor like a marble, gave me such vertigo I had to sit down and hold onto the legs of the chair not to faint. When it came time for Balbino and Hilaria to slaughter one of their pigs, whose rich, warm smell I had gotten to know over an entire summer, I was asked to hold the bucket to collect the blood, which they would later use to make blood sausage. Maybe as a *marrana* myself, I imagined some of my own blood filling that bucket. My hands shook so badly that some of the blood spilled. They laughed at me and took the pail away. I was no good even at that basic task. If the survival of the human race had depended on me, we'd all have perished.

SO WHAT WAS I GOOD FOR? I gave people in Santa María my respect. That was my purpose in being there. To give them the respect no one showed them, the respect they didn't give to themselves as confidently as they should have. Respect for their labor, respect for their knowledge, respect for their courage, respect for their stubbornness in staying rooted in a small place when the whole world had decided it was wiser to be in big places where money flowed like the ocean they'd never seen and you dreamed big dreams. As a daughter of immigrants and myself an immigrant child, I had so many abandoned places in my history I was no longer sure where I belonged, and yet destiny or chance had led me to a people whose feet were firmly planted in the soil of their own land and who weren't going anywhere.

All I could do on their behalf was write and preserve their stories and take their pictures. The only tools I knew how to wield were my pen, my typewriter, and my camera.

I set about documenting what I could of their lives. I didn't want a single moment lost to posterity. But I was a novice. I know I missed seeing a lot of things. I regret the stories that never made it into my fieldnotes. Stories I didn't know how to tell.

In such a small place like Santa María, I got to know all the inhabitants, some better than others, but in my mind, all these years later, I can still remember, house by house, from one end of the village to the other, those who lived there when I was a young woman, remember their gazes and their unusual names—poetic names like Venerable, Vitaliano, Laútico, Felicísimo, Dionisio, Apolonia, Aurora, Bonifacia, Justa, Saturnina.

I remember those who were infirm but were never treated as any less entitled to a full human life. I remember Nicanora, who had Down's syndrome, washing her own handkerchiefs at the fountain because her mother, Fuencisla, had tenderly taught her the importance of keeping them clean. I remember Fernando, a cognitively impaired man, who was cared for by his sister Inés and brother-in-law Sixto, poking the cows gingerly with his cane when he took them out to pasture. I remember the sweet smile of Aladino, confined to his bed because of a congenital illness that made his head too heavy for his limbs to support, cared for by his mother, Petronila, and by his siblings, Clara, Delmiro, and Amable, all of whom had a less debilitating form of the same illness.

I remember that everyone in the village showed David and me kindness. People gave us tomatoes from their gardens that tasted like candy. They taught us how to read the landscape of the village like a book; every path and hill and meadow had a name and a history. They let me photograph them, even when they were sweaty and tired. And they told stories. Many stories. About those who'd been blessed and those who'd been cursed, sad stories and funny stories, and stories that were sad and funny, like the one about their anxious priest, Don Efigenio, who feared he'd faint when he said Mass and had to be dragged to the altar by his cousin Sixto.

María, who took us in that first night, was a wonderful storyteller. She knew lots of proverbs. Some favorites were *Hay quién por cegar el vecino, se saca los ojos* (There are those who, wishing to blind their neighbor, gouge out their own eyes) and *Unos pa' cestos y otros pa' vendimiar en ellos* (Some are made to be baskets and others to drop their grapes inside them). It was David who wrote down these proverbs and María's stories in a little notebook, because his handwriting was better than mine and he was trying to learn Spanish. We often spent afternoons visiting María and would laugh remembering the assurance she gave us the day she met us, that she and Virgilio didn't plan to murder us in our sleep, and how she hoped we wouldn't murder them.

One day she told us a story about a pueblo where all the people wanted to be rich. God listened and sent an angel to grant everyone's wishes. The people were delighted. They rushed to the threshing ground to sing and dance because they were all going to be rich. And the angel arrived and everybody made a wish. The first person asked for sheep, lots of sheep. The next person asked for food, lots of food. The next asked for land, a lot of land. The next, for heaps of gold. And someone wanted lots of cows. All the wishes were granted. But then the one who asked for lots of food tried to find a servant to serve him his food, and of course, there wasn't anybody, because everyone was rich, so who was going to be a servant? The one who got the sheep couldn't find any shepherds. And the one who got the gold stood guarding it for four days, since he couldn't find anybody to help him bring it home. Finally, the one who had asked for lots of food went to visit the one who had asked for heaps of gold. The one who had gold asked the one who had food to help carry half of it, and he agreed. But afterward, the one who had gold had to help the one with food. He had to learn to be a servant too.

This was a fable about the kind of utopia that people dreamed of in Santa María: everyone had to help one another, and having gold didn't make you any better or more important than having food or sheep or cows or land.

Looking back, I was fortunate that the first place I went to in my travels as an anthropologist was to this village at the foot of the Cantabrian Mountains that my professor chose for me. It was there, among people who believed in a fundamental sense of humility and the worthiness of all human beings, that I realized I was on the right path.

After returning to Princeton, it was always a thrill to receive a letter from Santa María with 43 pesetas' worth of stamps bearing the wrinkled brow of King Juan Carlos. Sometimes the envelope carried a message: *"Recuerdos del cartero Abilio"* (Regards from Abilio the mailman). María wrote often, and there were also letters from Hilaria, Saturnina, and Sixto. They told us the latest news from Santa María and let us know who'd passed away. Occupied with working the land for most of their lives, they weren't in the habit of writing and would ask us to forgive the errors in their spelling. In closing, they always sent *"un fuerte abrazo de estos que no os olvidan"* (a strong hug from those who don't forget you).

I know this must have been one of the standard ways they were taught to end a letter, but I was always moved that they sent such words to David and me. When I replied, I always sent the same words back. And I really meant those words. I could never forget them. Never forget Santa María. It was a place of my youth. Where the kindness of strangers comforted me and gave me hope when I couldn't go home.

Doña Bartola in Mexquitic, Mexico, 1983.
Photo by Ruth Behar.

a gift from the women of mexquitic

....

After David made the decision to convert to Judaism, he and I finally
wed in 1982 in the Sephardic temple in Forest Hills, a few blocks from
my high school, under a chuppah of gardenias and with the blessing
of Rabbi Murciano from Morocco. My parents forgave me and welcomed David into the family. A few months later, summer gave way to
autumn. As the leaves fell from the trees, we loaded up the car with our
clothes and books and went to live in Mexquitic, a small town carved
out of the craggy hills in central Mexico. David had chosen to study
agrarian reform there for his dissertation. I accompanied him out of
a sense of fairness. After all, he had accompanied me for several years
while I did my dissertation research in the Spanish village of Santa
María del Monte.

The *presidente* of Mexquitic gave us permission to live in a munici-
pal warehouse. It stood on the outskirts of town, filthy and abandoned.
We could have it for a year or two if we fixed it up. At first we were miserable when we saw what they were offering: a long rectangular room
with a high ceiling, facing an enormous patio of broken concrete. On
the other end of the patio was the bathroom, a toilet with an adjoining
shower stall so close to the street you could hear the *Buenos días* and
Buenas tardes of people walking past. The bathroom lacked electricity,
and at night we had to find our way with a flashlight. Even during the
daytime I was afraid to shower alone. David waited outside the stall

while I bathed. He'd stand around patiently until I was done, then bundle me up in two towels he'd kept warm next to his chest.

We were twenty-five and felt we were still on our honeymoon. Slowly we turned the ugly warehouse into our nest. We found a used bed in the nearby city of San Luis Potosí. David bought wooden boards and built a table and a bookshelf. Wicker chairs from the market came next. At the FONART, the regional chapter of the national chain of handicrafts stores, I saw a wooden dresser embellished with hand-carved flowers and decided it was an extravagance we couldn't do without. Several yards of white gauze created a canopy over our heads.

On our two-burner electric stove we cooked beans and quesadillas, which we ate with avocados we divided in half. We were so in love that David always took the half with the pit so I wouldn't have to bother with it. At the market I found humble but beautiful Mexican plates made of red clay. We sipped sparkling Agua de Lourdes out of tall glasses rimmed in sky blue and pretended we were drinking champagne.

Our patio grew prettier each day. David cleared away the rubble, and I lined it with pots filled with orange geraniums and fuchsia bougainvillea.

I was living in Mexico, but I spent my days writing about Spain. I was a few chapters short of being done with my thesis. I stayed indoors and tried to force myself to finish quickly. A strange sensation—my head in one place and my body in another.

David ventured out of our nest each day and met the townspeople and brought back the news of whom he'd met and what he'd seen. I was so hidden, people joked with David that he kept his young wife locked up because he didn't want local men feasting their eyes on me.

Had we been in a city, no one would have cared about the foreign woman who could be seen now and then watering her geraniums. Neither a *gringa* nor a *mexicana*—it wasn't clear what she was.

One afternoon a group of six women came to our front gate, which we'd been instructed to keep locked at all times with a thick iron chain and a padlock, regardless of whether we were home. A local school-teacher named Sylvia led the group. Her light brown hair was trimmed neatly around her face. Intelligence shone in her eyes. The women were curious about me, the mysterious wife of the *gringo*. They'd come to say hello and see if I was doing all right.

I invited them inside, but they came in only as far as the patio. Sylvia said they knew I had work to do.

What kind of work was I doing that was keeping me so busy? she asked.

I said I was writing a thesis, and when I finished it and presented it to my professors in the United States, I would become a *doctora* in anthropology.

Sylvia smiled. "You must be very smart," she said.

Not at all, I thought. It was taking me too long to finish the damned thesis. I was plodding along, struggling to describe all that I had witnessed and felt in the village of my first fieldwork.

Sylvia was carrying a plastic bucket covered with an embroidered white cloth napkin, whose fringes were also crocheted in white.

"We brought you some tamales," she said.

Then she lifted the cloth; I could smell the warm corn and chili. It was all I could do not to reach in and eat one right then and there. Instead I invited Sylvia and her companions to stay and eat tamales with me. Politely they shook their heads. "No, these tamales are for you and your husband," Sylvia said. "We came for a short visit. We don't want to rob any more of your time."

I wanted Sylvia and the other women to stay longer. While I was sloppily clad in jeans and a T-shirt, they wore skirts that fell to their knees, handkerchief-thin blouses, and striped *rebozo* shawls loosely wrapped around their shoulders or folded on top of their heads to protect themselves from the scorching midday sun. I was enjoying their company, and the thought of having to lock myself inside and keep writing felt unbearably lonely to me.

At the door, Sylvia asked, "How is it you speak Spanish so well?"

"I was born in Cuba," I said. "But I've lived in the United States since I was a child."

"So you don't suffer when you cross the border. You can go back and forth without any problems."

"Yes," I said in a small voice. I hoped this admission wouldn't turn them against me.

The women took their leave, and Sylvia urged me to bolt the door shut. "It's safe here, but you never know," she said. "You're a woman and you're by yourself most of the day."

She waited until I was locked up inside to say goodbye and run to catch up with the other women.

I hurried back to our nest, closed the door, and tore into one of the tamales. Petals of the corn husk fell away. I savored the sweetness of the dough, the cleansing sting of the chili. I imagined the hands of the women who'd made these tamales, one by one. I ate another tamale and then another. Finally I sat down and began clicking and clacking at the keys of the manual typewriter. I was a fast typist. I'd learned to type without looking at the keys when I was ten and recovering from my broken leg. Eyes closed, half-dreaming, I wrote a lot that day. The taste of Mexico was in my mouth. I was more eager than ever to be done with my thesis and to come out of hiding.

IT TOOK SEVERAL MONTHS, but at last I finished and went back to Princeton to defend my work and receive my doctorate. On my return to Mexquitic the following summer, I scarcely spent any time indoors, instead going from house to house getting to know the women.

All of them had children, many children. If a woman couldn't have children of her own, someone, a sister, a cousin, gave her a child to bring up. To be a woman, you had to be a mother.

Sylvia, admired for being a schoolteacher who taught first-graders to read with the greatest of ease, was no exception. I watched her elegantly handle a household that included her mother-in-law, Doña Chonita, her father-in-law, Don Pedro, her husband, Manuel, who was also a schoolteacher, and their seven children.

One afternoon David and I went with Sylvia and Manuel to a fiesta in a nearby *rancho* that was being hosted by their friends. The mother of the family, together with all the women in the neighborhood, had spent a week grinding chilies, peanuts, almonds, sesame seeds, and chunks of Abuelita chocolate for the *mole*, to be served with tomato rice and tortillas. It was a warm and sunny day, but I noticed that Sylvia wore a wool serape that covered the front of her body. She was sweating from the heat and from the *mole*. Afterward I sat with her in the pickup truck waiting for Manuel and David to return so we could head back to Mexquitic. She took off the serape and explained that she was pregnant but didn't want anyone to know. Why? I asked. She told me that at thirty-eight she felt too old to be having another child. She hadn't expected to have any more. The pregnancy had left her feeling out of control.

At the end of the summer Sylvia's youngest daughter, Melissa, was born. She was a delight to the family and a surprise to the neighbors, who whispered playfully about how La Maestra Sylvia had kept her big tummy a secret from everyone. Sylvia lived in a large ancient house in the center of town that belonged to Doña Chonita. Even with the birth of yet another child, there was room enough and food enough and love enough to go around.

Most women in Mexquitic weren't so fortunate. Like the old woman who lived in a shoe, they had more children than they could house, feed, and love. Husbands yelled a lot and often beat their wives. Most men, old and young, deemed it beneath them to use contraception and refused to permit their wives to use it, because their manhood was expressed in their ability to father numerous children. Those women who had their husbands' permission to use contraception—usually an IUD—had to have the device removed when the men went across the border in search of work. If the wives had sex with other men while their husband was away, they'd get pregnant, proof they'd been unfaithful.

Isabel, the young doctor from the city of San Luis Potosí who was in Mexquitic doing her social service, was lonely and unaccustomed to living in the countryside. She felt as much an outsider as I, so we became friends. But like the women in Mexquitic, the *doctora* believed a woman had the responsibility to bear children. "You should have three children," Isabel told me as we relaxed in the white-walled office of the clinic after she put in a long day vaccinating babies. She was petite, demure, like a dove in her white scrubs, and I marveled at how efficiently she managed the clinic on her own. "This is why you need to have three. Having just one child is too sad. If you have two and one dies, you'll still only have one. Have three, and if one dies, at least you'll have two."

She'd spent so much time in the countryside that she'd seen many babies die from poverty and malnutrition. And yet, from what I could see, infant mortality was declining in Mexquitic, thanks to the concern for public health shown by people like the *doctora*. But Isabel also had a Mexican sensibility about life's fragility and knew that, at the snap of a finger, death could come swooping down and carry off anyone's beloved child.

One night Isabel sent a boy running to find me. "The *doctora* says you should come quick," he cried. "Don't delay." I was needed to help deliver a baby.

At the clinic the woman was about to give birth to her thirteenth child. Despite all the practice she'd had, she was weeping and moaning.

Isabel told me to hold the woman's hand and console her. Finally the baby slipped out, covered in a chemise of gook and slime, which the *doctora* said were pieces of the woman's deteriorating womb. It took me two hours to get the baby clean with cotton balls.

A few months later the woman became pregnant again. She had complications with the birth and needed to be rushed to the hospital in San Luis Potosí. At the hospital, without asking for permission, the doctors tied her tubes. She had been bearing babies since she was fifteen.

Her husband was furious. He raged at his wife, cursing and kicking her, convinced that the shutdown of her womb was a conspiracy between her and the doctors. Soon after, he abandoned her.

IN MY MID-TWENTIES, I FELT TOO young even to be thinking of having children, but the more I hung out with the local women, the stranger I felt about being childless. I wanted to tell them that I too had created something, not a baby of flesh and blood but a work of intellectual concentration, my doctoral thesis, into which I'd poured years of time and effort. A piece of my soul was lodged in that thesis too. I was scared and excited for this thesis of mine, which would soon exist independently of me. My professors had actually considered it good enough to be published. I couldn't find any way to say all this to the women in Mexquitic, to express to them the concept that it was possible for a woman to create life with her mind as well as her womb.

There was a woman in Mexquitic who'd call out whenever she saw David and me, "Adam and Eve, Eve and Adam! Are you two going to be alone forever? Who'll heat up tortillas for you when you're old?"

A woman I barely knew, sitting next to me at a fiesta, passed me a Coca-Cola and whispered, "I know a good doctor in San Luis Potosí who can help you if you're having problems getting pregnant."

When I was visiting a woman named Petra, she asked me my age and said, "What're you waiting for? The best time in a woman's life to have children is in her twenties. After you turn thirty your hips get hard and inflexible." She squeezed my hips with her palms. "*Ay Dios santo,* they're already tight. Don't wait much longer."

Then there were the legends of La Llorona, the Weeping Woman, who cried for her dead children, taken from her by the conquerors of Mexico or, in some versions of the story, abandoned or aborted by her and lamented too late. If you listened in the middle of the night, you could hear her wailing worse than a madwoman.

David and I had always used contraception. Neither of us knew whether we were fertile. What if, after our diligence in preventing a pregnancy, we discovered we couldn't have children? This question came to obsess me, and on one of our trips back across the border to Texas, where we went every six months in order to recross into Mexico and renew our visas, I picked up books about women's health, fertility, and pregnancy. I started keeping track of when I ovulated. I became aware of the days in the month when I might become pregnant if I let myself.

Meanwhile our grant money was running out. We had been in Mexquitic for nearly three years. Did we want to stay and become expatriates? We daydreamed about buying some land and building a house. But we had no savings. Trying to be practical, I sent out applications for postdoctoral fellowships in the United States. These were prestigious fellowships and I didn't have much confidence I'd receive any of them.

There was a *curandera,* a healer, in a neighboring *rancho.* I wanted to get to know her, but I'd been told she didn't want to be interviewed. She would see me only if I went to her seeking assistance for a genuine problem. She was famous in the region for giving men spiritual cleansings and talismans to help them get across the border safely. She lived in a shack that smelled of copal and frankincense and the marigold bouquets she kept on her altar.

I told the *curandera* I was worried about our future. I was waiting to hear about a job across the border. What if nothing came through? What would my husband and I do next?

She remained silent, gazing at me with unwavering concentration, which I found unsettling. Then she rose slowly. With her powerful hands, strengthened from years of extracting honeywater from the maguey plants surrounding her shack, she brushed me with some herbs, performing a *limpia* on me, a spiritual cleansing, and told me to pick three white flowers and place them under our mattress. I'd have my answer soon.

I did as the *curandera* instructed.

After a few weeks I forgot all about the flowers under my mattress.

ONE AFTERNOON I WENT TO VISIT an elderly woman, Doña Bartola, whom I'd gotten to know well. She lived with her daughter and granddaughter in the center of town. She was frail and suffered from tuberculosis, but she enjoyed telling me stories about her life. Her granddaughter sold *enchiladas potosinas* at the doorstep of their house twice a week, and David and I often stopped by to eat a plateful of these delicate chili-soaked tortillas, lightly fried and topped with chopped onions, grated cheese, and sour cream.

I ate the enchiladas and was invited inside the house to chat. David had an errand to do and said he'd return later. In one of the bedrooms off the central courtyard I found Doña Bartola sitting on a wooden bench. She motioned for me to sit on the bed. A baby, her great-granddaughter, maybe nine months old, was asleep next to the headboard between two pillows.

Doña Bartola and I conversed, not paying attention to the baby. After a while, the little one woke up and began to kick her feet and cry. Doña Bartola continued talking as if nothing had happened. "Her mother will attend to the baby when she's finished selling enchiladas."

The baby's demands for attention grew. She kicked her feet with greater urgency and her wails grew louder. Doña Bartola didn't budge. The baby's mother remained at the doorstep selling enchiladas.

Unable to bear seeing the baby unattended, I picked up the child and embraced her. Immediately she calmed down. I rocked her back and forth. After a while, I arranged the pillows to prop her up on the bed. She waited to see what I'd do next. I tickled her feet and she cooed with pleasure. Then she got tired and began fidgeting, so I picked her up again. Setting her on my lap, I rocked her up and down, up and down. Doña Bartola watched in silence. When the mother finally came to look in on her daughter, the baby was happily nestled in my arms. Feeling I'd done something helpful by attending to the baby, I was taken aback when the mother whisked her daughter away from me without saying a word. Soon after, David returned from his errand and we left.

The next morning another of Doña Bartola's granddaughters knocked on our door. She came bearing a message. "My grandmother needs to see you right away." I followed the girl to the house, wondering what emergency had arisen. At the door, Doña Bartola awaited me. She looked somber, as did the mother of the baby.

"The baby cried all night," the little girl's mother announced.

"I'm sorry to hear that."

Doña Bartola turned to me. "We think you gave the baby *ojo*. Will you please squeeze her head and wipe her with your blouse so we can be sure you didn't mean her any harm?"

I was shocked by this request, but I did as Doña Bartola asked. How could they imagine I intended any harm to the baby? I still felt they owed me thanks for entertaining the baby the previous day. But it turned out they thought I'd spooked the little one. Given her the evil eye. Hurt her with my longing and my envy.

Fortunately, by the next day the child had recovered. I was the one who felt anguished. By what right had I picked up a child who didn't belong to me and held her so close, so tenderly?

NOT LONG AFTER THAT INCIDENT, I went to get the mail from Doña Márgara. The post office delivered all the mail for the entire municipality to her store. I'd learned early on to stay on good terms with her, because if you weren't, she'd withhold your mail, tell you no one had written to you, tell you to come back tomorrow to see if you'd have better luck. I'd periodically buy a soda or a *bolillo* bun from her and pretend I wasn't in the least interested in the mail. She had a curious way of dealing with the mail. She'd dump the entire contents of the burlap bag on to the floor, then pick up the letters one by one and sort them.

I watched her painstakingly go through the mail as I sipped an orange soda. When she was finished, she casually passed two letters to me, which had been tucked between some bottles of cooking oil. "These are for you. They arrived yesterday."

The letters were responses to my postdoctoral applications. I opened them and couldn't believe it. I'd won not one, but two fellowships! The white flowers had given me their answer, just as the *curandera* had promised.

No, David and I weren't going to become expatriates, after all. There was a life, a purpose, calling us back to the other side of the border.

THE EARTHQUAKE THAT HIT MEXICO CITY in 1985 was brewing as we packed up the car again, filling it with all the Mexican pots and glasses we could squeeze in. We headed to Baltimore. I'd strung together a one-year fellowship at Johns Hopkins University and a three-year fellowship at the University of Michigan. We knew our destination for the next four years.

In Baltimore we sublet a house from an Orthodox Jewish couple. They got around the restriction of having to sleep in separate beds during the wife's menstrual cycle by placing two single beds side by side. David and I marveled at this arrangement. In those days, a single bed was big enough for the two of us. We slept in each other's arms all night.

I didn't notice it right away, but as time went on, I began to feel a little off-kilter in the mornings. I felt ravenously hungry, and yet when I tried to eat I couldn't keep anything down. I felt sad, I felt delirious. Everything inside me and around me seemed topsy-turvy. What was happening? Why did I feel drunk all the time? Were these physical sensations the result of my nerves? I was under pressure to appear smart and poised, to say brilliant things at the various academic events I was expected to attend. I needed to prove I'd been worthy of the fellowship and was experiencing a bout of impostor syndrome. Or perhaps I had a real illness—perhaps cancer was attacking my bones and blood?

I went to the local health clinic expecting to receive frightening news about my health. Instead I learned that the women I'd come to know in Mexquitic had worked their magic on me. I was pregnant. I was twenty-eight, two years to go before I turned thirty. My hips, I hoped, were still sufficiently flexible to allow me to carry a child.

Early in the pregnancy I suffered from nausea and headaches, but later I was relaxed and happy and no longer so worried about what my colleagues thought of me. David brought me breakfast in bed each morning—an omelet and toast. As my belly grew and I felt the baby kicking way up into my ribs, I knew my child was going to have long limbs. I got a burst of energy and became very productive, sending out for publication several academic articles about women's witchcraft in colonial Mexico, drawn from my reading of Inquisition records.

Summer began and we packed up. Before I left the rented house, I glanced back at the two adjoining single beds where our son had been conceived. I knew exactly the moment I'd gotten pregnant, when in the heat of passion we'd skipped the condom. How deeply I must have wanted a child! Our only swerve from contraception had resulted in pregnancy. Doña Bartola had seen that longing welling up in me before I'd recognized it in myself.

I drove our car all the way to Ann Arbor, Michigan. David followed in a U-Haul. We'd acquired more things and there wasn't room for them in the car. I barely fit behind the steering wheel. We stopped every two hours so I could go to the bathroom.

In Ann Arbor during the months of June and July, I cried every day. I'd wake each morning and weep. Maybe it was hormones. Maybe La Llorona was haunting me. Maybe I was crying out of fear of what would come next in my life. Could I become a mother and still read books and dream of writing my own? Would I be forced to give up the life I knew to attend to the little one's needs day and night? What did I know about being a mother? The world was full of dangers, everything from lightning and murderers to fires and ghosts. And what about the dangers, too numerous to name, hidden from view? Roses had thorns. Did I know how to protect my child from the evil eye?

I was so anxious that, when it came time to give birth, I couldn't let the baby out. I was in labor for three days. A midwife attended to me at the hospital and managed to convince the doctor not to give me a C-section. But the doctor had to wrest my child from me with forceps. In the past, they told me, I would surely have died in childbirth.

My son was born at exactly a minute after midnight. For several hours, I'd been clenching my teeth. My jaw was so stiff I couldn't speak. My tailbone cracked during the contractions. It hurt beyond words. Rage burst from my heart, rage at the universe, at God, for the body-breaking labor assigned to women since the expulsion from Eden.

Then my son was placed in my arms. Scratched and bruised from his perilous journey through the birth canal, he was awake and looked at me with eyes that seemed to say he knew, he knew what I'd been through, he understood, and he was sorry.

Had it been up to the women of Mexquitic, they would've sent me many more. But I decided to have only one child. When I returned later with my son and told them I was a *profesora* now and had to teach lots of students and read lots of books and write my own books in order to make a living, they nodded and tried to understand. At least, finally, I was a mother. I no longer posed a threat—I'd not gaze at any of their babies with a wolf's hungry eyes.

I've never stopped reading, and I have to say that the books I wrote after my son was born are far better than the thesis I wrote before he came into the world. I passed on my love of books to him. Now he's my most trusted reader and the wisest critic of the books I try to write.

My first thought when I looked back at my newborn child was that he seemed like a messenger from another world. And so I named him Gabriel. He was the most beautiful boy I'd ever seen. The women in Mexquitic had sent him to me. This angel. This gift.

the first world summit of behars

....

Early in 2004 a mysterious invitation arrived by fax from a man named
Iako Behar, a Bulgarian Jew living in Mexico. The fax announced that
Iako and his family would be organizing the first World Summit for
People with Family Names: Behar, Béjar, Vejar, Bejarano, Becherano.
Under this heading, it said, "September 6–9, 2004, a SUMMIT for the
above mentioned people will take place in the city of Béjar in Spain."
Participants could plan on hearing "a genealogy specialist talk about
the roots of and links between our names" and being given a tour of
the city of Béjar and the neighboring town of Hervás.

My interest was immediately piqued. On the basis of nothing more
than a flimsy fax from a total stranger who happened to share my last
name, I signed on to participate, eager to return to Spain and see it
anew from a Jewish perspective. Even before I did fieldwork in the
village of Santa María del Monte, I'd begun a relationship with Spain
in the months before I turned nineteen. At that impressionable age,
I went to Madrid for a semester study abroad and learned to smoke
Ducado cigarettes, drink sherry at sunset, and spend hours in the basement of the Prado Museum gazing at Goya's black paintings. It was
1975 and General Franco was taking a long time to die in the Pardo
Palace. Like a vampire, he was administered daily blood transfusions.
His grip on the Spanish people had weakened, but even then only a few
bookstores dared sell Hugh Thomas's critical history of the Spanish

Civil War. You had to ask for it at the front counter, and they'd hand it to you wrapped in brown paper.

When Franco finally breathed his last, the country let go of the burden of nearly forty years of dictatorship. Spain was ready to confront its history—its self-destructive twentieth-century history and the longer history, stretching more than five hundred years into the past, which shaped Spain into a homogeneous Catholic nation. Unified Spain, which became an empire that successfully carried out a massive spiritual and political conquest of the *Américas,* had been created at the cost of ridding itself of Jews and Muslims, most famously in 1492 but also before and after, through a relentless series of pogroms, wars, persecutions, and inquisitions. With Franco gone, democratization led to a desire to revive the memory of the Jews and Muslims who had once lived on Spanish soil.

This search for memory might have remained an obscure longing, were it not for the modern existence of the Sephardim, Jews who consider themselves exiles from Sepharad (or Sefarad) the Hebrew word for Spain, and feel an enigmatic, even mystical tie to the land that expelled them. Many Sephardim, dispersed throughout the United States, Israel, Turkey, and Latin America, speak to this day an ancient, musical, proverb-studded Spanish, called Judeo-Espanyol or Ladino, which to contemporary Spanish speakers sounds charmingly like the speech of Cervantes's *Don Quijote.* In fact the Spanish fascination with the Sephardim has a long history. In the 1880s Angel Pulido, a Spanish doctor and senator, discovered the existence of Sephardic Jews while traveling from Vienna to Budapest by boat. As he recounted in his book, *Españoles sin patria y la raza sefardí* (Spaniards without a Country and the Sephardic Race), first published in 1905, it was through a chance meeting with Enrique Bejarano, a Sephardic Jew who directed the Spanish Israelite school in Bucharest, that Pulido learned of Spanish still being spoken among those who'd been expelled. This encounter moved him deeply and inspired his lifelong quest to trace the Sephardic diaspora and help the Sephardic Jews return to Spain, a mission that failed to produce the redemptive ending he desired. Pulido felt the expulsion of the Jews had been an amputation, and Spain needed to recover, for its spiritual and material good, this severed limb of its history.

As a young woman, I hadn't yet read Pulido and was only vaguely aware of the historical transformations set in motion by the death of Franco. What I knew for sure was that Spain had captured my imagination. After my semester abroad in Madrid, I took a course at Wesleyan in which the only book we read was *Don Quijote*. The next semester I almost flunked out because I didn't study for my comprehensive exams, instead dedicating my energies to directing a theatrical performance of Federico García Lorca's *The House of Bernarda Alba*. I became an avid hispanophile, playing classical Spanish guitar, wearing Spanish capes and black felt hats, and speaking Castilian rather than Cuban Spanish.

Later I kept returning, in the late 1970s, throughout the 1980s, and into the early 1990s, to do fieldwork in Santa María del Monte. At a time when it was impossible to travel easily to Cuba, I felt I could lay claim to Spain because of my Sephardic roots. Those roots, I thought, were buried in the history of my last name, and I dared imagine Spain might be another of my lost homelands.

But my yearning for a sense of belonging in Spain came up against a stumbling block: I felt uneasy announcing I was a Jew, let alone a Jew with roots tainted by the expulsion. An anthropologist at the start of my career, I wanted to be accepted, and so I steeped myself in Catholic beliefs, rituals, and practices. Because I spoke Spanish and was from Cuba, people assumed I was Catholic. Every now and then, someone came right out and asked if I was Catholic, posing the question with a stern look, as if to say, "We sure hope you're Catholic," and I'd surprise myself and nod my head in agreement and change the subject. I never expected to have to lie about being Jewish. But the pressure to conform to a Catholic social order was huge. The rosary was recited daily in church. Sunday Mass was attended by virtually everyone in the village (the shepherd was excused, and one or two diehard anticlerical men). I suppose I might have refused to participate, but that would have been an act of disrespect. In the name of anthropology, I learned to recite the rosary in Spanish and to kneel at the appropriate moments in the Mass. I made the sign of the cross whenever everyone else did. I neither confessed nor took communion, but that didn't raise any eyebrows because only the village elders performed these acts of piety on a weekly basis.

In those early years of encountering Spain, I often wondered about the Behar name I'd inherited from my father and refused to shed, as American women do when they get married. Given that my father's family is Sephardic and had presumably lived in Spain five hundred years ago, could it be that we came from Béjar? I'd located Béjar on the map and noticed it was barely two hundred miles south of where I was in León, near the border with Portugal, in the region surrounding the famed university city of Salamanca. Intrigued, I took a trip to Béjar. I'm not sure what evidence I expected to find of my family's origins there, but maybe I'd get to see where the Jews had lived. In many Spanish towns and cities, it was becoming increasingly common for the old Jewish neighborhoods, called *juderías,* to be identified by plaques so visitors could easily find them. But when I went to Béjar, the city had yet to get its Jewish act together. I ended up roaming aimlessly through the streets and finally bought a souvenir, a keychain with an image of the Virgen del Castañar, the Virgin Mary venerated in those parts. The keychain sat on my bookshelf for years, waiting for that mythical key to appear that all Sephardic Jews are supposed to have kept to their long-abandoned houses in Spain.

INSTEAD OF THE KEY, IT WAS IAKO BEHAR who appeared with his romantic, crazy, far-fetched dream of organizing the first World Summit of Behars in the town of Béjar. But Iako was helpless to carry out his grand scheme without the technical wizardry of his son, Mario, and grandsons, Moris and Yaakov, who understood much better than he how to use the computer to scour the phone books in every part of the world. Thanks to the Internet's ability to annihilate geography and connect human beings, wherever they may be, Iako managed to send out 4,500 invitations to people with the Behar last name (and its derivatives). These Behars were Sephardic Jews, scattered around the globe.

My father, of course, received the same invitation I did, but he had no interest in going to the summit. "Go to Spain and meet Iako and his family," he said, chuckling. "I think it's going to be just you and them." By chance, it so happened I'd been asked to be a keynote speaker for a conference in London taking place immediately after the summit. My kind English hosts agreed to pay the slightly higher airfare that would enable me to make the stopover in Spain. Once I knew the trip to Béjar would be a gift, I figured I had nothing to lose. Even if I did nothing but sit around with Iako and his son and grandsons in Béjar, drinking sherry at sunset while musing on tales of our shared name, how bad could that be?

But as the date approached, it occurred to me that regardless of how few or how many Behars descended upon Béjar, this event was going to be worth documenting. I'd only recently completed *Adio Kerida / Goodbye Dear Love,* a documentary film about the Sephardic Jews of Cuba, which had done well for a first movie, traveling to film festivals around the world and landing distribution with Women Make Movies in New York, a highly regarded nonprofit company. Yet I'd vowed not to make another documentary—at least, not for a while. Making a documentary, I'd learned, was a time-consuming, money-losing operation, equally exciting and frustrating, as you, the filmmaker, went about madly seeking people who'd be honest, charming, deep, concise, and charismatic in front of the camera. After you'd discovered those people and fallen in love with them while watching them and listening to them hundreds of times in the editing room, it would then become necessary to cut them down to size in order to fit everything you needed to say into the space of a film sixty to ninety minutes long. No, this process had been far too unnerving, I told myself. Either interviewees stopped just short of saying something truly significant about what you wished they'd talked about, or worse, they'd say something beautiful and moving but there was no place for it in the story. I cried seeing good footage end up (metaphorically speaking) on the editing room floor. No more documentaries. Not for a while, anyway.

And still I was able to persuade myself that it would be relatively painless to make a short documentary about the World Summit of Behars. After all, the summit was going to last only four days. I popped an email message to Pepo, a twenty-eight-year-old filmmaker living in Madrid, to tell him I'd be in Spain for the summit. Just two years earlier, Pepo had found me by means of the Internet, and our renewed contact had blossomed into a strong friendship. I'd known Pepo as a child in the village of Santa María del Monte. His grandmother and mother, who didn't live in the village but returned during summers to maintain their ancient farmhouse, had warmly hosted me, and David and Gabriel, during my later visits. Pepo, it turned out, had been watching me do my research in the village, seeing me write down notes as people told me their stories and pull out my camera to snap pictures as they went about their daily lives. I learned that Pepo's interest in photography and film stemmed from the days he'd watched me, the foreigner, doing fieldwork, armed with an array of notebooks and cameras. When I emailed Pepo about the World Summit of Behars, I mentioned that I hoped to do some filming. He immediately volunteered to meet me in Béjar and be my cameraman. I told Iako of my plans to be in Béjar filming with Pepo, and he was enthusiastic about the possibility of a documentary emerging from the summit. From Iako's response, I assumed Pepo and I would be the only documentary filmmakers going to Béjar.

On my way to Spain, I wondered if our gathering would be like the one Alan Berliner documented in his film, *The Sweetest Sound,* produced in 2001, in which he brought together twelve other Alan Berliners from around the world for a dinner at his apartment in New York City to answer the question *Are there better Alan Berliners than I am?* Berliner also traveled to a meeting of the Jim Smith Society and the National Linda Convention to try to understand what it means to have a unique identity in our anonymous world. But something told me our summit would be different. We, the Behars, the Béjars, the Vejars, the Béjaranos, and the Becharanos, seemed to be on a more illusory quest: not simply to find out how we felt about holding a name in common but to uncover our lost home in a Sefarad that no longer existed.

AT THE BARAJAS AIRPORT IN MADRID, I'd been told by Iako to meet by the "Amigos" information desk. I was a little concerned that with these imprecise instructions I might not find Iako and the other Behars, but as I approached the central corridor, I knew I'd found my people. Atop a pile of suitcases on a luggage cart was perched a sign: "Behar Summit." I smiled and extended a hand. In the same instant, I saw myself caught in the flare and flash of cameras being managed by Iako's grandsons, Yaakov and Moris, who were simultaneously photographing and videotaping my arrival. As if this were not enough, Iako's son, Mario, snapped a quick picture of me with his digital camera as I greeted his father. It was clear this Behar father-and-sons team was not going to let a moment of the unfolding World Summit of Behars go undocumented. And we hadn't even made it to Béjar yet.

Already convened under the banner of the Behar Summit were a father accompanied by a son in medical school, Yakov and Ronen Behar from Canada, and four men, ranging from middle-aged to elderly, who'd come on their own: Craig Behar from Arizona, Bob Behar, a retired lawyer from Washington, Ezra Béjar, a botanical scientist from

California, and Marco Bejarano from Israel. I was beginning to fear I'd be the token woman and felt greatly relieved when Yehuda Behar, a retired colonel, arrived with his wife, Anat, from Israel, and Eugenia Behar from Mexico showed up with her niece, Mayra Behar, who was studying to be a chef. Ezra Behar, originally from Mexico, was drawn into conversation with Eugenia Behar, and the two soon realized that he was her long-lost nephew. Ties had been broken for decades after his father married a Mexican woman who wasn't Jewish and they'd moved to California. Ezra hugged Eugenia firmly, boyishly, and didn't let her out of his sight for the rest of the summit. This reunion of estranged kin was, as Mario later described it, "the first fruit of the summit efforts."

As we all stood exchanging stories, Iako said, *"Pueden sentarse por el mismo precio"* (You can have a seat for the same price). It was my first taste of his wry sense of humor. A retired electrical engineer, Iako appeared younger than his seventy-five years. He looked the way I imagined a Jewish Bulgarian socialist of a bygone era would look: he was short and sprightly, his cheeks were bright red, his white hair was a bit frizzy at the temples, and he was bald on top; he wore khaki pants and a pale beige shirt with the sleeves hastily rolled up to the elbows, as if ready to carry out any mission deemed necessary for the good of the people. And, sure enough, when he glanced at the large watch on his wrist and saw we were running behind schedule, he cried out, *"¡Vamos!"* Without further ado, he lifted two huge suitcases and as many smaller bags as he could hang on his shoulders and rushed out into the midday sun in search of the tourist bus he'd contracted for our trip to Béjar.

Once on board the bus, many of the Behars caught up on the sleep they'd lost in the course of their travels, including Iako himself. Mario, Moris, and Yaakov remained awake, indefatigably photographing and filming the entire three-hour journey. Everyone, absolutely everyone, had brought at least one camera on the trip. When we stopped in Ávila for our first group photograph, each Behar wanted his or her own copy of the picture, and fifteen digital cameras were pressed into service. As signs for the city of Béjar began to dot the edges of the highway, we scrambled to the front of the bus to grab the best pictures of that place-name, where we already felt certain we'd find a piece of ourselves.

We finally arrived, not in Béjar, but in that home away from home where all modern journeys begin: in a hotel. For its size and comfort and meeting halls, Iako had chosen the Cubino Hotel as the head-quarters for our summit, located on the outskirts of Béjar on a hilltop overlooking the city. Never had checking into a hotel been so hilarious an affair. One after another, we all signed in with the same last name. The hotel manager, José Montagut, a spry man with a perennial grin, who would become, for me, one of the most insightful commentators on our gathering, quickly got into the spirit of our Behar love fest and joked about how it was going to be very difficult over the next few days to announce a call over the p.a. system for someone named Behar.

Heeding Iako's call, a total of sixty-two Behars and their families soon converged upon the Cubino Hotel. People came from all over the United States and Canada, from Chile, Mexico, France, Bulgaria, Israel, and South America. At the opening reception on the outdoor patio, we swam in a Babel of languages. English, Hebrew, Spanish, French, Bulgarian, and our beloved Ladino—all these languages of our diaspora rose into the air and collided with one another. The late summer sun lingered in the sky and the night fell gently.

Pepo had arrived just in time, bearing a professional video camera he'd borrowed from a friend. He was eager to get started on our project, and though I was overjoyed to see him and grateful for his generosity and goodwill, I told him I was beginning to doubt it would be worth our effort to try to make a film about the summit. Why, I asked my-self, had I been so naïve as to imagine I'd be the only one who'd want to make a documentary? Two other Behars, Caroline from Paris and Andrew from Los Angeles, had come with identical plans and appeared much better equipped to carry them out. Caroline was a producer, accompanied by a professional camera and sound crew, consisting of five people hired in Spain, and she planned to use a vignette from the summit in a series she was preparing on the history of the Inquisition. With her flowing silk scarves always perfectly tied around her neck and her up-to-the-minute Parisian stylishness, she would surely produce an elegant and professional account of our gathering. Andrew, tall, athletic, handsome, said his previous films had been screened at Sundance, and he clearly had the savvy confidence, and apparently the contacts, to pull off making a film that would get noticed. Andrew had a terrific sense of humor and I imagined him turning our summit into a hugely entertaining comedy.

And so I told Pepo, there was nothing for us to do but throw in the towel. Even apart from these two fellow filmmakers, whose expertise I viewed as superior to mine, there was the Mario-Moris-Yaakov team, intent on jubilantly documenting everything. Then too no Behar had come without a camera. This gathering of Behars in the town of Béjar was simultaneously an ethnographer's dream and an ethnographer's nightmare. Some of the Behars, like Bob from Washington, had brought complex kinship diagrams extending back several generations, kinship diagrams of the kind I should have learned to produce in graduate school in anthropology but had failed to because, I must confess, the kinship class intimidated me and so I never took it. And many of the Behars had read extensively about the history of the Jews in Spain. Everyone was an expert, everyone an ethnographer, but none of us was sure what we'd do if we actually found evidence proving we were from Béjar.

Perhaps, I thought, the most original thing I could do would be not to record anything, not to create any documents, but to commit what I felt to memory, to my imagination. But Pepo looked at me so sadly when I shared these doubts with him that I couldn't bear to disappoint him. "Let's try and see what we can do," he said, with that cheer in his voice that I so adored about him and also adored in his mother's voice. He turned on the camera and off we went to the crowded outdoor patio where all the Behars were happily mingling.

It was an ideal time to capture on tape the range of pronunciations that people used when introducing themselves. Behar could be pronounced "Be-har," with a very soft *e*, but I also heard "Beehar" and "Bayhar." And the accent shifted between the first (Bé-har) and the second (Be-hár) syllables of the name. Across the board, everyone pronounced the *h* in the name as if it were the strongly aspirated Spanish letter *j* (think "José"), even though the letter *h* itself is always silent in modern Spanish pronunciation. Our ancestors had spelled their name using the Hebrew alphabet, which was used for writing Judeo-Espanyol or Ladino. Only long after the expulsion from Spain, in the early twentieth century in countries such as Turkey, did they begin commonly to use the Roman alphabet, as it was used where they lived. This explains why virtually all the Behars present at the summit spelled their names with an *h* rather than a *j*. But Andrew Behar, who'd put away his camera, explained how he'd deliberately streamlined the pronunciation of our name by removing the *j* sound, so as not to have people puzzling over the name when they heard it for the first time. "I tell people my last name is 'Bear.' And they ask me, 'Bear'? I tell them, 'Yeah, like grizzly. But with an *h* in the middle.' 'Oh, okay.' That's it. Simple. Done."

The excitement of being around so many diverse people who shared the same last name still didn't make any clearer what exactly we were all doing in Béjar. No one was certain of our exact mission. Had we all responded to a narcissistic temptation? Did it really make sense to journey to Spain from so many parts of the world just because we shared a last name with one another and with a Spanish city nestled in the snow-capped mountains near Portugal? What did we want to find in the present-day Spain that had expelled our ancestors five hundred years ago because they'd chosen to hold on to their Jewish identity rather than convert to Catholicism by order of the Inquisition? Were we on a heritage quest, or on the first stage of an angry political journey to demand our acres and mules?

Among the first people I pulled aside for an interview about these matters was a lively young man, dressed casually in shorts, sneakers, and a T-shirt, who had the same first and last name as my father: Alberto Behar. A student in economics at Oxford, Alberto had been born in Israel and raised in South Africa. He spoke perfect Spanish; his mother, Marta, was from Argentina, and his father, Leon Behar, from Colombia. Marta and Leon, still living in South Africa, had accompanied Alberto to the summit. When Pepo turned on the camera, Alberto chose to speak in his South American–accented English: "Usually people ask me where's my name from. Hopefully after this conference, or summit, or whatever we wish to call it, I'll be able to come up with an answer. If you go back far enough, the Hebrew word *behar* is, of course, mountain. That's what I used to tell people. And then I was told, 'No, that's the wrong story; you need to tell them that actually it's from Spain, that it's from the Inquisition, that we left Spain.' So that's the story I'm running with now." Turning and pointing to the snow-capped mountains behind him, Alberto added, "Hopefully I'll find out something interesting about this place, where apparently we're all from."

While Alberto envisioned our summit as a quest for the appropriate narrative about the origins of our name in the city of Béjar, other participants wanted something more concrete to come of their journey to Spain—they hoped to find the house, the street, or at least the neighborhood where their ancestors had lived and, if nothing else, to stand where their ancestors had stood, to be a witness to history. For Claudia Behar from Paris, being in Béjar was about claiming the dignity that her father and mother, Sephardic Jews in Egypt, had tried so hard not to lose by clinging to an image of themselves as Spaniards at a time when they felt they had no country.

Andrew Behar, the filmmaker from California, had come with his cousin, Richard Behar, an investigative journalist in New York City, who planned to help Andrew produce his documentary. Richard was charming and affectionate, taller than Andrew, but lanky, with only the slightest stoop in his posture from years of writing. He put a brotherly arm around my shoulders and told me I could stay at his Greenwich Village apartment whenever he was away traveling. As the inaugural dinner was being prepared, we went inside the hotel to a quiet corner of the dining room, where tables were set with china and silverware and wine glasses were waiting to be turned right side up.

Pepo turned on the camera, and Andrew began. "When I got the fax, I thought it was just a come-on for money. You know—like "Buy your family crest.'"

"Yeah, genealogical spam," responded Richard.

"But it just sort of stuck in my brain," Andrew continued. "A couple of months later, I looked at the fax again and I realized they're not trying to make money, because there's no connection to airfare, and all that other tourist stuff."

Andrew then forwarded the fax to Richard, who lost it, and finally Andrew lost his copy as well. By August the two had decided they'd go to Béjar, but as Richard remarked, "We were surfing through the Internet and couldn't find the summit anywhere, and we thought this couldn't be real, because why wouldn't there be a website you could get to through a Google search if it was real?"

Richard had found me on the Internet and emailed me to see if I was attending, and I confirmed that the event, as far as I knew, was "real," and that I planned on going. I connected him again to Iako.

Both Andrew and Richard had sketchy memories of their Turkish grandparents from Ankara. They'd grown up in the United States and hadn't even met each other until they were teenagers. They joked that they didn't know what they'd do if they met any long-lost relatives at the World Summit of Behars. It was hard enough managing the relatives they already had, let alone getting everyone together for Thanksgiving. Richard thought all the participants in the summit ought to give a vial of blood, to have their DNA checked and "make the links." As he put it, "We'll never find out whether or not we're all related by trying to decipher scrolled-up yellow pieces of paper from Ankara that no one can make out anymore." Andrew's comeback to this was, "I'm sure Béjar is just full of DNA blood specialists!" He joked, "Maybe the testing will reveal that *we're* not even related!"

Even though they were both bemused about our gathering, the cousins had read up on the history of the Jews in Spain and spent time in the archives in Madrid before the summit. "We've been doing some research—when did the Jews come to Spain, who were the Sephardics, when was this genocide, when was that genocide," noted Andrew. "The reason we're in Béjar is because this one king said, 'Let's not wipe them all out. We need to have some commerce, some lawyers, some doctors.' He gave them sanctuary here, until his granddaughter Isabella finished it off with the expulsion and the Inquisition. We know our relatives were living in this town."

As I later verified, Andrew was right about Béjar's having been a final refuge in Spain for Jews pushed out of larger towns and cities in Castile and Andalusia in the violent century leading up to 1492. Whether he and all of us Behars had ancestors from Béjar was more difficult to determine, even though he was certain of it. Andrew was truly furious about the loss of Spain and had a vivid personalized image of the expulsion. He described men arriving with swords and horses and killing half his ancestors and telling the surviving half to get out of the country. Pointing out the window, he exclaimed, "I feel like my great-great-great-great-grandfather lived in that house right there. That house, right there." Sephardic Jews, he felt passionately, were owed compensation, at the least Spanish citizenship, in return for the suffering their ancestors had endured.

BUT NEITHER COMPENSATION NOR citizenship was ever mentioned by the local officials who witnessed and celebrated our return to Spain. Béjar's mayor, Alejo Riñones Rico, a compact, hardy man, who in another era would've been cutting wheat with a scythe, announced how pleased he was to have us "back" and joined us for dinner at the inaugural first evening at the hotel, where we were served whole fish because José Montagut, the hotel manager, had been told that Jews could eat neither pork nor fish that had been cut. José was befuddled not only by Jewish dietary laws but by the fact that all of us had traveled such a long distance to be present at the summit. "From South America, all the way here to Béjar!" he exclaimed. "Just because there's a meeting with other people of the same last name?" He said he couldn't possibly imagine traveling thousands of kilometers for such a meeting. Then he laughed. "Maybe I should try it with my last name," he said, but he clearly thought the idea absurd. Not only was the summit inconceivable to him but the notion of being so utterly mobile, of not batting an eye at the thought of getting on a plane to some place so far away, jarred his sense of his own rootedness. In his life he'd moved between the poles of Béjar and Barcelona, extremely different and distinct places but both in the same country. Yet he spoke of the necessity of boosting Béjar's tourism industry and said he was not about to complain if Behars from every part of the globe wanted to visit.

The next morning we were all invited to the city hall, where the mayor again greeted us, this time under a large smiling color photograph of King Juan Carlos and Queen Sofia. He spoke of how we carried the name of the city proudly throughout the world, and that in this way we, a group of Sephardic Jews, served as ambassadors of Béjar.

It was a curious fact that in the city of Béjar there weren't any Béjars or Behars; the name had become, in almost all instances, a patronymic of the Jewish diaspora. Town residents were called Bejaranos in Spanish, much as in English we say someone from New York is a New Yorker, but this was not a last name. Our being named Behar connected us inextricably to the place called Béjar, and it was from this perspective that the mayor welcomed us to the city which we "should never have left." He proclaimed the day historic, for we had returned to Béjar "to walk the same streets our ancestors had walked many centuries ago." As soon as the mayor finished his speech, we all filed out into the plaza and stood before the cathedral, and a group photograph was taken for the story to appear the next day in the local newspaper.

The date of our summit, it turned out, had been set for early September to coincide with the opening of a Jewish museum in the city of Béjar. The construction of the museum was supposed to have been subsidized by the city and the regional council, but they ran out of funds. To complete the project, they'd turned to an individual, David Melul, a Barcelona Jew of Moroccan origin, who was willing to make a major donation. Melul had studied engineering in Béjar in the 1940s and he felt a close bond with the city. In those years Béjar was a thriving textile center, with dozens of factories scattered around the outskirts of the city by the shores of the river. Melul's father worked in the textile business and had many contacts in Béjar. As a young man Melul had been well received there, and he was glad for the opportunity to assist in the completion of the museum and that the museum should bear his name.

After the event at the city council, our group meandered down to the edge of the old city, huddled against its stone fortress walls, where the new museum had been built. It was there that the *judería,* which I'd been looking for on my earlier trip to Béjar, was said to have been located. Our group and many local residents squeezed into the tiny plaza at the entrance and watched as a mezuzah was placed at the entrance of the museum. Melul recited the blessing in Hebrew, and the assembled Behars, in addition to townspeople, repeated the words after him. This was the only ritual of a religious nature conducted during the summit, for none of us was particularly observant. Then Melul and other dignitaries entered the museum, oblivious to the fact that, as soon as their backs were turned, the mezuzah slipped off the wet cement and fell to the ground, breaking in half. I feared this might be a bad omen but was consoled when David Behar, an Israeli, told me it was like the breaking of the glass at a Jewish wedding, said to mark the memory of the destruction of the Temple in Jerusalem, a custom which Jews practice to balance the joy of the present with the sorrow of the past.

Once all of us were inside the museum, both the mayor and Melul unveiled a plaque covered by the Spanish flag. The plaque indicated that the inauguration of the museum "took place in the presence of Jews, descendants of those forced to leave in 1492, whose last name marks their connection to the city from which they were separated for five hundred years and with which they are now reunited." José Luis Rodríguez Antúnez, the architect, who was dressed in a dandyish beige suit and exuded caffeinated energy, then went on to explain the design of the museum, inspired by the Diaspora Museum of Tel Aviv, which he'd visited as part of his research. He told us that the Jewish museum in Béjar had three floors and that the third floor was empty, waiting to be filled by our memories, the stories of our diaspora. On the main floor, a room with a glass floor was to be the starting point. The room was not yet completed. The architect explained that the plan was for people to enter this room, in the dark, and to hear the Edict of Expulsion read to them in the resounding voices of Ferdinand and Isabel as if they were Jews in Spain in 1492. With the appropriate sound effects and the glass floor covering a deep pit, museum visitors would feel the ground quaking under their feet and find themselves forced to make the decision of whether to stay and convert, or to leave Spain and go into exile. He hoped museum visitors would put themselves in the shoes of the people who had to make that decision five hundred years ago and decide what they would do. Those who chose to stay would proceed through the museum and learn about the history of Béjar after the expulsion; those who chose to leave would skip that history and go directly to the top floor, to that room that was yet empty, waiting to be filled with the stories of our Sephardic diaspora.

As an architect Antúnez had put a great deal of thought into the design of the museum. Clearly it will eventually play an important role as a learning center for Spanish schoolchildren, who he envisions will visit the museum in groups. But it will be some time before that reality comes to pass. The opening of the museum had been rushed so that it could coincide with our summit. It was mainly a shell of a building, filled with a map of Spain indicating the areas where Jews had lived and a copy of a Jewish tombstone found in Béjar, the original having been taken to Toledo for safekeeping years earlier. In his speech, Antúnez said the museum was waiting for our contributions—spiritual and intellectual—but after some prompting he added, with a bit of embarrassment, that it was also much in need of our financial support.

Richard Behar had jokingly said to me that, before the summit ended, our hosts would find a way to make us take out our checkbooks. Exactly as he'd predicted, at the lunch following the museum opening, the new director of the museum announced a series of price brackets, in which donors would occupy different positions, depending on the size of their financial contribution, in the new hierarchy of patrons of the museum.

That evening the city of Béjar regaled us with a concert of Sephardic music, a Middle Eastern dance performance featuring local children, and a dramatic reading of the Edict of the Expulsion presented by a male and a female actor. After five hundred years, the edict issued by King Ferdinand and Queen Isabella, with its harsh words warning Jews "not to linger in Spain or risk certain death," had somehow become a form of entertainment. I wondered if Spaniards saw the edict as being as much a part of our Sephardic heritage as our music and our dances. In 1992 King Juan Carlos, wearing a skullcap, had apologized for the edict at the Calle Balmes Synagogue in Madrid and asked for "forgiveness" for the "cruel and unjust" events of five centuries earlier. But after our evening program ended, it was impossible not to realize that we were still in a deeply Catholic country. As we headed out into the cool night, a live band and fireworks filled the central plaza, for it so happened that our summit had also coincided with the annual fiesta for the Virgen del Castañar, the Virgin emblazoned on the keychain I'd brought back from Béjar years before.

Spain was at a crossroads, filled to capacity with immigrants from Latin America, Africa, and Eastern Europe, about whom native Spaniards felt intensely ambivalent. It seemed that the construction of a Jewish museum in Béjar, the elaborate attention the mayor of Béjar was giving to our summit, and the night of Sephardic entertainment prepared on our behalf were meant to demonstrate that the search for Jewish and Muslim memory that had begun after the death of Franco was taking place in earnest. And yet I kept wondering whether the official and touristic interest in bonding with the living and breathing Sephardim had made much of an impact on everyday Spanish life.

From his position behind the camera, Pepo had taken it upon himself to ask people in Béjar if they knew any Jews and whether any Jews lived in Béjar. Over and over, people would reply that no, they didn't know any Jews, and they certainly didn't know any Jews living in Béjar. When Pepo approached a group of elderly men with his questions, one of them pompously announced he didn't know any Jews, but he was certain there were many in the world, because, as he put it, there are many more Jews out there than there are *gente buena,* good people. Pepo was stunned at such a raw anti-Semitic response from a fellow

Spaniard. It consoled him when another elderly man, whom he approached next, replied that while he didn't know any Jews, he was sure he had to be "a little bit Jewish," because Jews had been in Spain for such a long time.

From the moment of our arrival in Béjar, the bus driver and other locals who didn't feel the need to court us, let us know that the town's textile industry was going through hard times. Most of Béjar's textile factories had shut down. Only a handful were still functioning and producing the famous Spanish woolen capes that continued to be worn by the king and queen. Young people had been forced to move to Madrid and other cities, part of the same exodus one finds throughout Spain. In summertime, during the fiesta, Béjar grew lively, but in the wintertime, I was told again and again, you won't find a soul in the street after eight o'clock at night.

Responding to the double crisis of economic and population decline, the officials in Béjar appeared to be turning to Jewish heritage tourism as one solution to their problems; they were also building a textile museum in an abandoned mill and expanding the ski resort. If one looks at the growth of packaged tours to "Jewish Spain" in the past several years, it seems that the Spanish government in general hopes to cash in on the growing Jewish interest in traveling to Spain to search for Sephardic roots. It's not an exact parallel to Jewish heritage tourism to Poland, where travelers visit the Warsaw Ghetto and death camps, which critics refer to by the painful term "Shoah business," but there's definitely a Sephardic travel boom taking place, an "expulsion business," which extends well beyond the usual trip to Toledo and Córdoba, as shown by our own summit in Béjar.

While it hasn't happened yet, it may well come to pass that one day Béjar will be a touristic Jewish stomping ground, like that which can be found already in the neighboring town of Hervas, which our group of Behars visited, as we'd been promised in Iako's original fax.

But Hervas was sadly Disneyfied, with its so-called Jewish tavern, its freshly mounted street signs in Hebrew, and its gray-pebbled Star of David etched into the plaza leading down to the old *judería*. Which was worse, I asked myself: to confront the loss of the traces of the Jewish past in the landscape of Spain, or to impose fake markers of Jewish memory, as they'd done in Hervas?

THE DAY BEFORE OUR SUMMIT ENDED, a Mexican Jewish genealogist, Alejandro Rubinstein, was invited to speak to our group and provide insight into the origins of our name. His skin was pale from spending too much time indoors, and he looked studious with his wire-rimmed glasses. I had a chance to speak to Rubinstein shortly before his formal speech to the group, and he told me he was concerned that his listeners wouldn't be happy with what he planned to tell them. The essence of what he had to say was that most of us, if not all of us, wouldn't find our roots in Béjar. It was doubtful whether even a handful of Behars derived their name from the city of Béjar. The majority of us, he was certain, had gotten the name because of its Hebrew meaning, either *bechor*, meaning "first-born," or *bachar*, meaning "chosen people." Jews who had been expelled from Spain, he explained, took pride in having held on to their Jewish identity under dire conditions and felt chosen to spread their traditions to other parts of the world. Many of us were Behars because our ancestors considered themselves to have been so chosen.

When Rubinstein made his detailed PowerPoint presentation to the members of our group, he urged all the Behars present to feel honored that our ancestors had chosen their namesake because of their love for their identity, their faith, their history. This, he insisted, was much more important than whether our ancestors were actually from the city of Béjar. But he went yet further in his assertions, maintaining that not all of us necessarily had ancestors who'd come from Spain. The

Behars in the room protested and said that of course we were all from Spain—hadn't our ancestors spoken Ladino? Rubinstein responded by saying that there were Ashkenazi Jews who migrated to Turkey in the nineteenth century from Eastern Europe and assumed Sephardic customs, but they weren't true descendants of Spain.

The genealogist was a party pooper, pouring cold water on the imaginary homeland we Behars were creating with the full cooperation of Spanish officials. Could we trust him? Not only was he not a Behar, he wasn't even Sephardic. Here we'd come, from all different parts of the world, to find our roots in the city that bore our name, and he wanted us to go home and tell everyone we'd made such a long journey in vain. Not only might Béjar not be indisputably ours; even *la Espanya* was possibly no longer the lost country we could grieve over and long for.

I was concerned that the joyful spirit of our World Summit of Behars would dissipate and that people would feel disappointed by the expert opinion rendered by the genealogist, who supported his claims with seventy references at the end of his presentation. But I discovered that my fellow travelers on this journey to Béjar were resilient and resisted surrendering to Rubinstein's studied claims. They acknowledged his greater expertise, but they weren't convinced he was necessarily right.

On our last night in Béjar we turned the camera on the young Behars who'd come to the summit, who I imagined would be more susceptible to the academic power of the genealogist's assertions. Ronen Behar, the medical student from Canada, acknowledged that the genealogist had presented seventy references, but all those references could be wrong. Ronen saw through the mask of scholarship and observed that, essentially, all scholarship is partial, never the whole truth. He said it seemed so Jewish, so Talmudic to throw everything into doubt and to seek various and contradictory explanations for things, instead of being happy with one answer. He concluded that we'd come to Béjar thinking we were from Béjar, and why should we change our minds now, just because the genealogist had a contrary opinion? After five hundred years, it was going to be difficult decisively to prove one theory or another, so he thought that ultimately you should go with "what's in your heart." And in his heart, Béjar and Spain belonged to him, and he didn't plan to let them go. Even if he didn't speak Spanish or Judeo-Espanyol, his Spanish origins remained very real to him.

Moris Behar, the grandson of Iako, who had dark melancholy eyes, agreed with Ronen. "To me it doesn't matter if my family wasn't born here four or five centuries ago. If they were born here, great, I have a connection, but I already have a connection with the family name. You can't live your life, if someone tells you something, constantly asking yourself, 'Did he tell me the truth or did he tell me a lie?' Sometimes you've got to believe."

All the Behars seemed to feel as did Ronen and Moris. They weren't about to accept the idea that in the end, Béjar might have nothing to do with us.

But later that night I spoke to David Behar, whose Bulgarian family had resettled in Israel when he was a child. He now worked in telecommunications and had a well-traveled air about him. A fellow insomniac, he preferred to talk rather than sleep. He grudgingly admitted that he had to agree with Rubinstein; we'd found little in the city of Béjar that was directly related to us—there was the Jewish museum and the name of the city, but everything we'd seen was contemporary, nothing that tied us firmly to the past and to history. Nevertheless, he said, lowering his voice to a whisper, we should keep this secret to ourselves and confidently return to all of our homes in so many different parts of the world and announce that we'd found our roots in Béjar.

Perturbed, I asked, "So you want us to tell a lie?"

He replied with a playful wink, "Well, who knows? Maybe it's the truth."

It was almost dawn. In a couple of hours we'd all be leaving. But we Behars could keep our peace of mind. We had convinced ourselves, more or less, that we hailed from the city of Béjar. Now we could travel light, letting ourselves be blown back to our scattered destinations, like the dry leaves the September winds were starting to shake loose from the trees.

unexpected happiness in poland

When Baba died in 2000 at the age of ninety-two, the only inheritance I wanted were her books: the books by Sholem Aleichem, Isaac Bashevis Singer, and other great Yiddish authors that I couldn't read, and the Danielle Steel novels I'd never read, everything. My family didn't mind; no one else wanted them. At the time, I also grabbed The Book, the handwritten memoir of my great-grandfather's youth in Poland that he wrote after settling in Cuba, which I so fervently wanted to keep. And with much less fanfare I happily acquired one more book of magical proportions: the Goworowo memorial book, which Baba had shown me a few times. It documented the story of her Polish hometown, which was just north of Warsaw, close to Treblinka.

After Baba's death, I pretty much forgot about the Goworowo memorial book. It stood untouched in my home in a special bookcase with stained-glass doors reserved for my most precious books. In December 2006, preparing for my first trip to Poland, I remembered I had this book in my possession. With a little key I unlocked the bookcase, took down the book, and leafed through the pages. Aside from a map of Goworowo and a brief introductory note in English, the book was in Yiddish. It contained photographs of Jews who'd lived in the town, both those who'd perished in the camps and those who, by the time of publication in 1966, had found new homes in Israel, the United States, and Canada. Turning a few silky pages whose edges had been folded and refolded by my grandmother, I came across photos of my great-grandfather Abraham Levin. He'd participated actively, I learned, in the creation of the book.

Poland had never interested me, in large part because Baba had always said she had no desire to return there. But it was at three o'clock in the morning, and being an insomniac who makes unexpected decisions at an hour when most people are sleeping as soundly as babies, I decided to travel to Poland. I invited a former student of mine, Erica Lehrer, to accompany me on the six-day trip. Everything I knew about contemporary Poland I'd learned from her. Erica's dissertation, which I'd supervised, was a sensitive interpretation of the sad, hopeful, and surreal collisions between Jews of Polish descent and Catholic Poles that have occurred over the past twenty years as a consequence of American Jewish and Israeli heritage travel to Poland. Prior to World War II, 3.5 million Jews lived in Poland, turning it into a major center of Ashkenazi culture. In post-Holocaust, post-Communist Poland, where Jews numbered only a few thousand, the return journeys of the descendants of those who'd perished had unleashed an ironic marketing of the Jewish past. Erica had brought to my attention the creation of Judaica tourist kitsch, including wooden "Jewish dolls" decked out in Chasidic white shirts and black coats.

The night before we left, I told Erica about my grandmother's book.

"Oh, good, you have the *yizkor* book for Goworowo," she said. "*Yizkor* books exist for hundreds of towns where Jews lived in Poland. They're an amazing resource."

Yizkor means "may God remember," and the *yizkor* ceremony is a remembrance service to bless departed family, neighbors, and martyrs. I'd been taught by my mother to run out of the synagogue during the Yom Kippur *yizkor* because she'd always heard it was bad luck to be there as long as your parents were alive. Back then, Baba and Zayde still lived, and she'd grab my hand and pull me away before the chanting began. Now, with Erica, I learned a new meaning of *yizkor*, associated with the books that sought to keep alive the memory of the victims of the Holocaust.

"I'll photocopy the map and the English introduction," I said. "The book is heavy. I don't want to lug it all the way to Poland."

"Bring it," Erica urged me. "There may be something in the book that will guide us on our trip."

Up until the last minute, I was ready to leave the book behind, though I had no qualms about cramming a pair of high-heeled black boots into my suitcase. With Erica's help, I'd arranged to give lectures in Warsaw and Krakow about my research on the Jews of Cuba and was vain enough to want to look elegant for those public events. As I left the house, I still resisted, telling myself the photocopied English pages would suffice for my purposes. Then I turned back and grabbed the book.

Two days later, a tall man with dark curly hair and an anxious look about him, Waclaw, our driver and guide, led us to his vw van and said, "Today on your Sabbath we shall go to Goworowo." Waclaw had never been there, but he'd been to dozens of similar towns with Jewish clients. He considered himself "a friend of the Jews" and said his non-Jewish Polish friends often criticized him for being too supportive of Jewish causes and the state of Israel. "I really believe that Poland lost a lot, losing the Jewish community," he told Erica and me. "Poland lost intellectual potential. It wasn't just a loss to the economy. Jewish people contributed so much to this country."

When we pulled into the town, Waclaw stopped before the sign for Goworowo so I could snap a photo. Just before we reached the plaza we passed the church, which my grandmother had described as huge, especially compared to the modest wooden synagogue now erased from the landscape. At the main plaza, we turned and crossed the bridge, hoping to find the remnants of a Jewish cemetery. A man in the town pointed vaguely in the direction of a field and said maybe something remained there, so we parked the van and looked around. All we found was black earth that had just been plowed and mushrooms sprouting in the marshy footpaths.

Disappointed, we headed back to the main plaza. I'd brought the memorial book with me, and we turned to the page with the map to get our bearings. In the plaza there was supposed to be a memorial to the Jews who'd been killed during the war, but it was gone. Instead there was a large monument dedicated in Polish to "all" who had suffered under the German occupation.

A few men were gathered around a bench. "I want to speak to them," I said. "Maybe they can help." Erica felt apprehensive about my request, but Waclaw, viewing me as a client he had to please and with a measure of his own curiosity as well, approached one of the men and inquired whether he knew anything about the Jews who'd once lived in Goworowo.

"That was a long time ago," said one man. "Before I was born," he added, turning away brusquely, as if offended. Another man looked at us with unadulterated contempt. "There are plenty of Jews in the government—go ask them." He too then stalked off.

But the third man, who was older and wore a cap that didn't quite cover his wrinkled forehead, stepped forward, eager to tell us a story from his childhood: how he once missed morning Mass and went swimming in the river, getting his clothes drenched, and how he'd knocked at the door of a Jewish neighbor, who tried to iron his clothes, but scorched them, then offered him new clothes, which he refused, for fear his father would beat him for skipping Mass.

Before us, at the bus stop, were a handful of people who looked "modern": a woman with a nice leather handbag, a young man with a knee-length wool coat. What to say to them? What to say to anyone in Goworowo? I wanted to show them the memorial book, show them the pictures of the Jewish people who'd walked these streets along with their ancestors, but I didn't dare. The Jews of Goworowo had turned into ghosts, and that appeared to be how the present-day residents wanted them to remain. All that was left of the flesh-and-blood Jewish presence was inscribed in the *yizkor* book I held in my hands.

I was suddenly overwhelmed by the futility of this visit—to come all this distance to look at a hometown my grandmother had had no desire to see again. To do something useful, I took pictures of the plaza, the streets, the houses, the bridge. At least now I knew the place my grandmother had dreamed of leaving. Surely that was enough. Even after Waclaw charged me a minor fortune for his services, plus an additional charge per kilometer traveled, I told myself that I'd been blessed to be able to return.

On Monday morning I was scheduled to meet with Anka Grupinska, the director of Centropa, an organization in Warsaw that documents contemporary Jewish life in Central and Eastern Europe. When she asked me why, exactly, I wanted to meet with her, I told her I was looking for the Polish Jewish roots of Cuban emigrants. And then I told her about my personal interest in Goworowo.

Minutes before setting off to meet Anka, I checked my email. She'd sent me a message at the crack of dawn, with the subject "surprise surprise." I opened the message and discovered an attachment: an interview conducted in 2004 with a man named Yitzhak Grynberg, which had been part of Anka's work for Centropa. Mr. Grynberg was a Jew from Goworowo! He had an excellent memory and was brimming with stories. His wife had told Anka that she didn't bother using their address book to find friends and family; she simply asked her husband, who kept everything in his head.

Anka, it turned out, was warm but solemn. She'd spent many years uncovering hidden Jewish lives. We talked like old friends about a dozen different things, sharing our passion for oral histories. I thanked her for the interview with Mr. Grynberg and told her I wanted to meet him.

"He's eighty-six," Anka said. "I don't know if he's still alive. But I'll look for his phone number and call him tonight." She paused for a moment. "And what language will you speak to him? Do you speak Hebrew or Yiddish?"

I shook my head.

Mr. Grynberg could speak eight languages, but English wasn't one of them.

"Does he speak Spanish?" I asked.

Anka brightened. "Yes. He lived in Spain for many years."

Mr. Grynberg was indeed alive. On the phone, he spoke beautiful Spanish and told me it would be a pleasure to talk with me about Goworowo.

"I have a marvelous memory," he said. *"Una memoria maravillosa,"* he repeated, accentuating each syllable. "I can tell you everything about Goworowo." He paused and added, "I can also take you to Goworowo and show you where all the Jews once lived, where the synagogue was located, where the cemetery used to be. I have a marvelous car. *Un coche maravilloso. . . .* I would be happy to drive you there myself."

Erica and I had made previous plans to visit Krakow so I could give a lecture and meet some of her friends. It wasn't until two days later that a taxi dropped me off at Mr. Grynberg's building in Warsaw. I found the elevator and was greeted at the front door by a small man with ruddy cheeks and glowing eyes. *"Venga, venga,"* he said, ushering me inside with the zest of a leprechaun. Mr. Grynberg bore a resemblance to Baba's three younger brothers, my great-uncles. And he too seemed to see something familiar in me. On the phone, I'd told him my great-grandmother, Hannah Gallant, was from Goworowo. "I remember the Gallants," he'd said. Now, as he looked at me, he said, "Yes, definitely, you are from the Gallant family."

His wife, Krystyna, an elegant woman wearing a brown pantsuit, her blonde hair coiffed at the beauty parlor, her nails freshly manicured, emerged from the kitchen and took my coat. Mr. Grynberg told me to make myself comfortable on the sofa. From a cabinet on the other side of the room he pulled out three passports. He showed them to me—Polish, Spanish, and Brazilian—all of them current.

"I have lived all over the world," he said.

At the outbreak of World War II, he'd fled Goworowo with his mother and father and his younger siblings. His father died of exhaustion before they crossed the border into Russia, but he and the rest of his family waited out the war there. In 1946 he and his family went to Israel, and from there he went with his wife to Brazil, where she and their son were killed in a plane crash. Afterward he found it too painful to remain and left for Germany, where he met Krystyna and remarried. The Grynbergs vacationed in Spain, liked it so much they settled there, and opened up a restaurant. Eight years ago he retired and returned to Poland with Krystyna. She isn't Jewish and still has family in Warsaw.

"Things are better now for the Jews in Poland," he said. "Not like before. I don't hesitate to tell anyone I meet that I'm Jewish."

The phone rang, and Mr. Grynberg began speaking in Hebrew to the person on the other end of the line. It was the rabbi from the Orthodox synagogue, he explained, asking whether he'd be attending services.

"I read perfectly in Hebrew," Mr. Grynberg declared after putting down the phone. "Not like some of the other men, whose Hebrew is mixed with Yiddish and Polish. That's why the rabbi always wants me to come for the minyan. But I told him I can't be there today."

Mr. Grynberg came back to his seat across from me on the sofa. I glanced out the window at the pale sky.

"Will we have time to go to Goworowo today?" I asked, knowing the answer.

"It's too late," he said. "It will be dark soon. If you had come at eight in the morning, we could have gone. But we can go tomorrow, if it's not snowing."

"I'll be leaving tomorrow," I told him sadly.

"What a pity you didn't call me sooner!"

I explained that I'd only just learned of his existence. To console him and also to console myself, I put the Goworowo memorial book in his hands.

He looked at me in amazement. "You have the book!" He held it close to his chest for a moment before yelling out, "Come, Krystyna, look!"

Krystyna came rushing in from the kitchen, wiping her hands on a dish towel.

"It's the book from Goworowo," he said to Krystyna. Turning to me, he asked, "How did you get this?"

"From my grandmother."

"It's been many years since I've seen it. I left mine in Brazil. I'm so happy to see the book again! All the Jews who lived in Goworowo are here in the book!"

He took a deep breath. As if by magic, he opened it to a page that made him gasp, then he dropped his head into his hands and began weeping. Krystyna stood by his side, gently caressing his cheek.

"These are my parents, Gedale and Hannah," he said, still weeping, and pointed to two pictures arranged side by side: a bearded man with a cap and a woman in a white-collared dress. Krystyna left the room and returned with a glass of water and a pill. When his tears stopped, Mr. Grynberg ran his hand over the picture several times. Then he turned the page.

He leafed through the book and paused every so often to comment. He laughed when he saw the photograph of Shlomo, the town fool. "He was not well in the head, but he delivered water to the houses, like you see in this picture, with his two buckets, and everyone loved him." His smile faded. "Ay, ay, ay, Shlomo Akiva, what became of you!" I feared he would weep again. Just then, Krystyna entered with a tray of tea, cheesecake, and pastries like Baba used to make, which we called *mariposas*—crispy, butterfly-winged slivers of dough dusted with confectioner's sugar.

"Come," Krystyna said. "Let's have tea."

I devoured one *mariposa* after another, forgetting to ask what they were called in Polish, while Krystyna poured cup after cup of tea.

Mr. Grynberg asked if I had time to stay for an early supper. I told him yes. I had the entire afternoon free.

"Qué maravilloso," he said. "I only wish I'd known before. I would have made a Jewish meal for you. With gefilte fish."

"And kreplach," I added, suddenly nostalgic.

He smiled. "Kreplach? I make kreplach that are *maravillosas!*"

It had been years since I'd eaten them, but when I was a girl, Baba had made them often, those Jewish wontons that were a little too thick to melt in your mouth but tasted heavenly either boiled in soup or fried after the broth had run out.

"We'll make something good for her," Krystyna said, and a few minutes later she excused herself and went off to buy food for our meal.

Mr. Grynberg and I returned to the sofa, sitting so close I could feel his every breath. He scoured the book page by page, testing his memory by looking at the pictures and seeing if he could recognize faces before reading the text in Yiddish. A book had never felt so utterly precious to me before—so powerfully capable of awakening emotions.

At the sight of old friends, Mr. Grynberg's eyes lit up, and he called out their names, as if trying to summon them. He sang aloud in Yiddish when he saw a page of lyrics and music. He looked for pictures of my family, checking on every page for the Levins and Gallants. He found relatives I'd never known were there: my great-uncles Moshe and Eleazer and my great-grandmother Hannah Gallant's parents and siblings. He read aloud slowly from the list of names of all the Jews from Goworowo who'd been killed during the Holocaust; seven were Gallants, including my great-great-grandparents. And he wept again, more desperately, when he came upon a picture of an older sister who'd perished in the Warsaw ghetto with her husband and three children.

"How young and beautiful she was, my sister! This picture, please make a copy and send it to me," he said, wiping his eyes. He shut the book and held it close to his chest, as if it were the dearest thing in the world.

Suddenly I worried I'd done him harm by appearing out of nowhere with the book. Had I stirred up memories that should have been allowed to lie dormant?

But Mr. Grynberg assured me that the book only reminded him he'd been young once—reminded him of a time before he'd wandered the world, living in many places, learning languages; reminded him of a time when Poland was his only home, when speaking only Yiddish was language enough.

"Take good care of the book," he said. "I never thought I would see it again."

In the midst of our conversation, Krystyna had quietly come home and made supper. She called out to her husband, "Can you help me, please?"

Mr. Grynberg went to the kitchen and I followed. He removed a pot from the stove, carefully lifted a slab of meat, and lowered it onto a chopping board. He sliced the beef thickly and said it was all for me and him, that Krystyna preferred chicken. Most of the time I too would have preferred chicken, but I ate the meat, along with the salad and boiled potatoes Krystyna had prepared. When I was done, Mr. Grynberg put another slice of the beef on my plate.

"Do you live well?" he asked.

"Very well," I said.

"There is nothing you're lacking?"

"No," I replied, wondering where the question was leading.

"If I can ever help you, please promise you'll tell me. You're sure you don't need money?" he asked with a look of such concern I almost wanted to say yes to please him.

"I have this apartment, and I have another apartment that's empty," Mr. Grynberg continued. "When are you coming back to Poland?" he asked.

I didn't know when I'd be back. I hadn't expected ever to be back. I'd thought of Poland as a one-time destination. But maybe now there was a reason to return.

Mr. Grynberg appeared to read my mind. "Well, don't take too long," he said. "Next time you're coming to Warsaw, call me in advance. I will wait for you at the airport. And you will stay here with us, or at our other apartment—wherever you like. Bring your husband and your son. You won't need to spend any money when you come the next time. No hotels, no restaurants. I know you paid a fortune to go to Goworowo. But with me, it won't cost you anything. I will drive you there myself in my own car."

I thanked him. I didn't want to leave, but night had fallen hours ago. I asked if I could use their phone to call a taxi. Mr. Grynberg said it wasn't necessary. He would take me back to the hotel himself. He and Krystyna had tickets to the Yiddish theater, and my hotel was on the way.

Mr. Grynberg still had the strength to throw open the massive doors of the garage, which was just big enough to fit his car, a vw Passat, the very same car I drive in Michigan. As we drove, I realized that he and Krystyna lived only a few blocks from where I was staying in Warsaw. I could have walked to his apartment. He'd been so close.

The Goworowo memorial book was nestled safely in my bag. This book, which had felt heavy in Michigan, this book I'd been so reluctant to bring with me, now felt like the only thing in the world that had been worth carrying to Poland.

Mr. Grynberg sang in Yiddish as he drove through the streets of Warsaw, and Krystyna sang along with him, their voices harmonious and unburdened. I was almost afraid. This was more happiness than I'd dared imagine possible in Poland.

part three

CUBAN GOODBYES

*the freedom to travel
anywhere in the world*

....

I first met Danayda in 1993 in Havana. Is it correct to say that I met her? She was only a child, just four years old, holding her father's hand. I knew José Levy, her father, fairly well by then, and he'd brought Danayda to a Hanukkah party at the Patronato Synagogue. We'd greeted each other and after the party we hung around chatting outside. Danayda was clasping a teddy bear. There were no teddy bears for sale in Cuba at that time; even now they're difficult, perhaps impossible to find in any store on the island. The teddy bear was a Hanukkah gift from an American Jewish mission that had come to Cuba to bring donations of medical supplies and gifts for the tiny Jewish community that was in the early stages of revitalization.

As we stood in front of the synagogue, we watched the visitors from the mission climb into an air-conditioned Havanatur bus and drive away. I'd been a passenger on one of those luxurious buses more than once. I knew what it was like to ride tall, above all the people meandering along in the heat or sandwiched together on a crowded bus. I knew the relief of being released from the heat and grime of the tropics, and I knew that Levy and Danayda had never had the privilege of touring the city that way.

I glanced at Danayda with her teddy bear. She looked adorable, her hair done up with pink and turquoise bows. I asked Levy if I could take her picture and he said yes. She didn't look like her father. He had pale white skin and pale green eyes, and she brown skin and brown eyes. If I had to date the start of my relationship with Danayda, it would go back to that day, when I gazed at her through the viewfinder, snuggling with the teddy bear that had come to Cuba as an act of charity.

I was in Havana, on my own, searching for the Jews who stayed on the island that my family had abandoned. My parents and Mori and I had lived half a block from the Patronato Synagogue. From the two bedroom windows of our old apartment, we could see the pastel blue arch of the synagogue, a jubilant flair of its 1950s modernist architecture. There's a picture of me as a little girl standing in front of the pink stone façade, decorated with bronze symbols of the twelve tribes of Israel. As I took Danayda's picture, I was well aware that I was reenacting my childhood picture. I'd been that little girl once, in a different historical and political moment.

Built on the eve of the Revolution of 1959, the Patronato Synagogue included a library, dining room, and social hall and was intended to serve as the community center for the 15,000 Jews who lived on the island in that era. Jews had prospered in Cuba after fleeing anti-Semitism and poverty in Europe between the world wars. Afraid to lose their culture, they married within their Jewish ethnic circles. Unions between Ashkenazi Jews from Eastern Europe and Sephardic Jews from Turkey were rare. Those few who dared to marry outside the tribe were ostracized. Crossing the color line for most Jews of that generation was simply unthinkable. A child of Danayda's color wouldn't have been seen in any synagogue in Cuba in the 1950s. The island community was now ethnically and racially mixed, no longer obsessed with the social distinctions that had been so central to the Jews who'd built the synagogues they'd barely had time to enjoy.

The Jews had initially supported Fidel Castro. But their enthusiasm waned as properties and businesses were quickly nationalized, posing a threat to their livelihood as shopkeepers and merchants. Even street peddling became illegal under the Communist system. Many feared their Jewish identity would be at risk after religious schools were closed and atheism imposed on the nation. The majority chose to leave in the early 1960s. Only a few chose to remain. Some supported the Revolution. Others had strayed from the Jewish tribe after marrying out and didn't want to be uprooted.

José Levy was among those who remained. The son of a Sephardic father and a Catholic mother, Levy worked in the merchant marine in the 1960s and 1970s, spending time in the former Soviet Union. On his return to Cuba, he grew disillusioned. He tried to leave the country in 1980 during the Mariel exodus but was apprehended by the police. The years that followed were dark and angry. Then in the late 1980s he found solace in attending religious services at Chevet Ahim, the first synagogue built on the island, founded in 1913 by Sephardic Jews. Praying next to the Bay of Havana, he didn't expect ever again to sail on the boats that came and went.

Divorced from his first wife, with whom he'd had a daughter, Levy moved to Havana's Chinatown. Across the hall from his apartment lived Florinda. They were married briefly, and Danayda was born of their union, a child of the crossroads between Afro-Cuban and Jewish Cuban culture. She'd grow up in her mother's home, together with her half-sister, Omni, ten years older and the daughter of a different father. But Levy would bring Danayda up as a Jew, though children inherit their Jewishness from their mother, literally from the womb of their mother.

Danayda was born in 1989, the year of the fall of the Berlin Wall, and she came of age in the first years of the new century, a post-utopian moment. The "special period" of the 1990s was in full swing when she was a child, a time of shortages, hunger, and moral crisis in Cuba. In response, Fidel Castro opened the country to tourism and made it easier for Cubans abroad to pump money into the economy through their remittances. There was no stigma anymore in expressing one's religious faith. Catholic and Protestant churches, Jewish synagogues, and Santería temples opened their doors. After decades of state-enforced atheism, Cubans flaunted crucifixes and Jewish stars and dressed all in white after initiation into Santería.

Once God was allowed back, the U.S. government sought to encourage religious freedom by facilitating travel for Americans going to Cuba on humanitarian and religious missions. Anthropologists like to say that once a country is featured in *National Geographic*, it's safe for Americans to visit. Cuba passed that test: a cover story, "Evolution in the Revolution," appeared in 1999, and it sparked a flood of American travel to Cuba that has not stopped.

The religious missions brought Bibles as well as aspirin and medical supplies, powdered milk, clothes, computers, and other goods that helped Cuba cope with the economic crisis. More frivolous items, like the teddy bear Danayda received, also arrived on the island after decades of limited access to material goods.

In 1992 the American Jewish Joint Distribution Committee in New York began to offer financial and educational support to rebuild Cuba's Jewish community. *El Joint*, as it came to be known, sent teachers to educate people about Jewish religion and history, and rabbis to perform circumcisions, conversions, and weddings. Most Jews, being of mixed background and having received no religious education, knew little about their Jewish heritage. The aim was to bring them into the fold of the Jewish international community. As soon as *el Joint* entered Cuba, other American Jewish organizations followed, eager to help save the remaining one thousand Jews.

The idea that a handful of Jews still lived in Cuba under Communism seemed astonishing to American Jews. This miniature Jewish community was instantly hailed a "miracle" of Jewish survival, a lost tribe in need of being rescued. When American Jews travel to Poland with March of the Living, or on their own, they visit the Warsaw Ghetto and concentration camps in Auschwitz and Treblinka, sites of destruction and trauma in which their ancestors perished, journeys deep into the heart of grief. But the journey to Cuba resonates with joyous images of cigars, mojitos, salsa dancing, and pristine beaches. Unlike Poland, which American Jews regard as a country that maligned Jews and aided the Nazis in their extermination of the Jewish people, Cuba is seen as a multicultural Caribbean island where Jews were never persecuted. American Jews may be loyal supporters of Israel, but they consider it a dangerous country, whereas in Cuba the likelihood of being killed in a suicide bombing is close to nil.

As the Jewish revitalization in Cuba took off, I watched as the Patronato, the synagogue I associated with my interrupted childhood on the island, became the headquarters for the comings and goings of American Jewish missions. In the early 1990s the roof was caving in. Pigeons flew in and out through the broken windows. But by the year 2000 the synagogue had been lavishly restored by "Jewban" exiles; they'd made their fortunes in Miami and didn't expect to return to Cuba but still couldn't bear to let the synagogue of their youth fall to ruins. They sent over a million dollars and had their names engraved on a plaque by the entrance.

Sadly, the oldest synagogue in Cuba, the Chevet Ahim, had to be shut down because money for its restoration never materialized. José Levy took it upon himself to move the Torahs from Chevet Ahim to the newer Sephardic synagogue, the Centro Sefaradí, located a few blocks from the Patronato. He'd become the president of the Sefaradí, after struggling to get the building back from the government, which had turned it over to the Ministry of Culture. There was a spacious sanctuary, much too large for the existing community, and Levy allowed it to be used as a rehearsal space for the musical group Síntesis. The airy room next to the office became a gym where exercise and yoga classes were offered. Levy collected rent for the use of these spaces to pay for the upkeep of the synagogue. He turned what had been the women's meeting room into the new sanctuary. He taught himself Hebrew and became versed in biblical commentary, leading services on Friday nights and Saturday mornings, at first painstakingly, but eventually with greater ease. He nurtured a loyal group of congregants, mostly elders with a sprinkling of young families.

For Danayda, the Centro Sefaradí was a second home and a magical place where American Jews appeared, bearing gifts. They brought mezuzahs that attracted good luck when placed on the doorposts of one's home; they brought menorahs with colorful candles to light on Hanukkah; they brought golden Jewish stars on delicate golden chains; they brought Hanukkah "gelt," little wafers of chocolate wrapped in foil and stamped like coins. She spent her childhood sliding down the ramp leading from the entrance of the building to the synagogue office, where her father sat reading all day. It was always a treat to see what surprising things had arrived from the world beyond.

As she grew up, she paid closer attention at the religious services, led by the men, who carried the Torahs up and down the aisle to be touched and kissed. A fading color picture hung in the office showing Danayda amid a group of old men holding nine Torahs brought from Turkey, her little girl's brown face in a sea of white faces. That was how she grew up, in the company of Jews who looked nothing like her but with whom she shared a common history.

DANAYDA LIVED ON A STREET WITH MANY potholes, but this is common in Centro Habana. Her building was dilapidated, but the neighbors kept it clean. A long flight of stairs and a path through an outside hallway led to her home. It was modest, but its tall ceiling allowed Florinda to build a second story, a *barbacoa*, or a loft, as these additions are called in Cuba. On the wall hung a framed picture of

Danayda wearing a blue dress, her hair tied in pigtails. It had been air-brushed; her smile was angelic, her cheeks rosy.

All my interactions with Danayda had taken place in the Centro Sefaradí. It wasn't until the summer of 2000, when I was working on my documentary, Adio *Kerida/Goodbye Dear Love,* that I went to her home. She was eleven by then. I interviewed her, asking if her friends knew she was Jewish. She replied that they all knew and that she was proud of her identity and her faith. Later I filmed her with Levy, who was teaching her to read in Hebrew from the Torah scrolls in preparation for her bat mitzvah. I admired him for challenging patriarchal traditions and passing on sacred knowledge to his daughter.

The following summer I spent more time visiting Florinda, Omni, and Danayda in their home in Havana's Chinatown. Florinda is a Jehovah's Witness, as is her oldest daughter, who is married and lives apart with her three children in a nearby building. An aspiring salsa singer and performer, Omni, the middle daughter, had a regular gig at a popular restaurant on La Rampa, a major thoroughfare in Havana. She'd been initiated into Santería and played the drums and chanted for the *orishas,* the deities of the religion.

I marveled at how Florinda, Omni, and Danayda coexisted in a single household, although each believed in and practiced a different religion. The ease with which they lived together and respected one another's faith seemed peculiarly Cuban, and in filming them I sought to convey their tolerance for cultural diversity. What I didn't know at the time was that I was catching a fleeting moment in their lives. A few years later they would be flung apart, as first Omni and then Danayda succumbed to the seductions of globalization, both becoming part of the growing number of young women who choose to migrate in search of the prosperity and happiness that elude them at home.

When I returned to Cuba in December 2001 for the premiere of *Adio Kerida/Goodbye Dear Love* at the Havana Film Festival, Danayda came to the screening with her mother. Omni came with an Italian boyfriend. I worried about what they'd think of the opening segment of the film, a nostalgic collage of pictures of myself as a child walking on the oceanfront Malecón with my mother and father, accompanied by a voiceover about my search for home in Cuba as a returning immigrant. The film is titled after a Sephardic song about pining for a lost love, and the lost love in this case is the island of Cuba. At the time of the screening, these romantic sentiments were not yet part of the lived experience of Danayda, Florinda, and Omni. But it wouldn't be long before they too would learn firsthand about the longing for home of those of us in the diaspora.

On my return to Cuba in 2002, I hoped to talk further to all three women. I climbed up the familiar stairs to their apartment and was surprised to learn that Omni had departed a few months earlier.

"She's in Poland," Florinda announced.

She'd been discovered by a Cuban salsa leader who heard her sing on La Rampa. He lived in Poland and had invited her to perform in his band.

Her mother recounted to me how Omni had written her a long letter soon after arriving in Poland. Her trip had been awful. It was the first time she'd traveled on an airplane. She carried a notebook filled with goodbye messages from her mother, her sisters, her nieces and nephews. She read them over and over and wept all the tears she hadn't wept when they saw her off. Finally she fell asleep, and when she awoke, she learned that her flight from Cuba to Amsterdam had arrived late, and she'd missed her flight to Warsaw. She didn't know who to ask for help. People were rushing in all directions. God, am I crazy? Omni asked herself. Why had she left her home for a country she didn't know, a language she didn't know, to work with people she didn't know? She saw that there was an information desk. But the woman at the desk couldn't understand her. Omni banged on the counter with her fists and yelled, "Español, Español, Español." The woman finally dialed a phone number and put her through to someone who could speak Spanish. Exhausted, Omni reached Warsaw, where members of the salsa band were waiting for her.

Fortunately afterward everything had gone well. Her subsequent letters were exuberant. She wrote about her apartment, her television, and the plush rugs you could set down on the bathroom floor and actually step on, unlike the old rags they used in Cuba. She told Florinda and Danayda about the shopping malls that had many shoes and clothes to choose from. And everything smelled new.

Omni sent photographs; in one she looked like a movie star. Dressed in an elegant red wool coat and tall black boots, she stared into the camera fearlessly. Tears came to Florinda's eyes as she showed me this photograph. She said she knew it wasn't right to be sad. Her daughter was fulfilling her dream. Who was she to stop her?

Danayda, by then thirteen, glanced wistfully at the photograph. "Doesn't my sister look beautiful?" she said. "She could never have worn a coat like that in Cuba."

AS THE YEARS PASSED, DANAYDA OBSERVED many of the Jews she knew from the Centro Sefaradí leave Cuba for Israel. They left secretly in the early 1990s through a plan called Operation Cigar, but subsequently they left openly and in larger numbers. Taking a raft to sea in the hope of landing in Miami was a desperate option that many disaffected Cubans chose. But Cubans who could claim Jewish ancestry had Israel as an alternative destination in the developed world. By making aliyah, literally "ascending" to the Jewish homeland, Cuban Jews received free housing and a stipend during their first year as immigrants. Soon Danayda saw her uncles depart, then the younger brothers of her father, with their entire families, and her half-sister, the daughter of her father's first wife, also left. The philanthropy of the American Jews had created a hunger for economic independence and social mobility. Every few months Danayda saw her father use a red pencil to cross off names on the membership list for the Centro Sefaradí. He didn't plan to leave, but he didn't stand in the way of those who wanted to.

After Omni left, Danayda could think only about the day she'd leave Cuba too. Israel had become a concrete place to set her dreams upon. Day after day, she looked out the window of her mother's apartment, as if seeing Cuba for the last time. When asked to write a high school report about any country in the world, she chose Israel. This took courage; her teacher espoused the official government policy on Israel and was vehemently anti-Zionist. If pushed to discuss her plans for the future, Danayda said she wanted to leave. Her future, as she envisioned it, was not to be in Cuba.

Florinda and Levy tried their best to get Danayda to stay put. Her mother reminded her about the good things the Revolution had achieved; there was free health care, and Cuban children didn't beg in the streets. Her father reminded Danayda there was no going back if she changed her mind. He reminded her that being an immigrant wouldn't be easy. He reminded her that there was no need for her to leave: she had food, a roof over her head, the Centro Sefaradí.

I too listened apprehensively to Danayda. I worried that my own presence in her life was a bad influence on her. She saw me come and go with a freedom she lacked. Much as I wanted to reclaim my roots in Cuba, I was a walking billboard for the immigrant success story. Was it hypocritical of me to tell her not to leave? My own family had left Cuba and gone to Israel before settling in the United States. Why wasn't I encouraging her to follow the same path?

I began to think she was watching me as closely as or even more closely than I was watching her. When I started out in my career, all the people I observed as an anthropologist were older than I, old enough to be my parents, or even my grandparents, and it was their memories of the past that interested me. With Danayda, I was trying to imagine her future, something that had yet to be.

During the years I got to know Danayda, I was already a mother. She is only three years younger than my son. She could be my daughter. Saying this, I realize Gabriel grew up in Michigan amid my absences as I returned obsessively, trip after trip, to Cuba. Seeing Danayda each time I went had anchored me. I cared about her. So I worried about her.

In those years while she was waiting to leave, Danayda lost her limber girl's body and became voluptuous. She could feel the heat of men's eyes on her flesh when she walked down the street. She knew that young women with her mermaid hips and brown skin could sleep with a Spanish or Italian tourist and in a few days make enough money to buy a television. But Danayda couldn't see herself using her body that way. At the age of seventeen, she decided to marry her boyfriend, Carlos, ten years older and not Jewish. As soon as they married, she and Carlos applied to leave for Israel. Her father said she'd married Carlos because she didn't want to immigrate alone. Possibly he was right. Danayda never imagined her father would give up the Centro Sefaradí. It was his life. He'd spent all his waking hours there for fifteen years. But one morning Levy made his decision: he'd leave too. He had held her hand when she was a little girl going to the synagogue, and he would hold her hand when she was grown up and going to the Promised Land.

I FELT SAD THINKING THAT DANAYDA AND LEVY would soon be leaving Cuba. I knew I had no right to feel that way. I selfishly wanted them to remain, to be there always, while I continued to flutter to and from the island. As I was pondering their departure, upon my return to Michigan I made a sudden decision to go to Poland with Erica Lehrer. I emailed Omni to let her know I'd soon be there and wanted to meet. How had Danayda's beautiful and talented older sister fared in a country I associated mainly with the Holocaust? I was eager to find out. But Omni didn't respond to my message. I worried that perhaps she wasn't doing well, that the seductive pictures she'd sent home to Cuba were just a cover. My gloom deepened as I visited sites of suffering in Poland. With Erica, I went to the Warsaw Ghetto. Then to Treblinka. Next to Krakow. Erica had been to Auschwitz before and she didn't want to go again. So I went alone. No one should go to Auschwitz alone.

On my last day in Krakow, I happened to check my emails and saw a message from Omni. She lived three hours away and was coming to see me. At midnight she arrived at my hotel. I expected her to be decked out in her glamorous red wool coat and high-heeled boots. Instead she was wearing jeans, a down jacket, sneakers, and a baseball cap. Omni had left her Italian boyfriend. Her Cuban boyfriend, a drummer named Ariel, had immigrated to Poland to be with her. He had shining eyes and restless energy, even standing still. Just hugging the two of them lifted my spirits. I felt overjoyed to hear the rhythmic cadences of their Cuban voices. But they were both bilingual now. The hotel receptionist did a double take when they greeted her in fluent Polish. Her gaze lingered on their black skin.

I led them into the lobby where we talked breathlessly. The hotel's bar was closed, so we decided to go out for a drink.

We walked fast. It was freezing in the middle of the night. Groups of Polish men were carousing outside the bars. Omni and Ariel tensed up. Omni whispered, *"En la calle tenemos que estar a cuatro ojos, a la defensiva todo el tiempo."* (If you're black, you need "four eyes"—you need to be on the defensive.) "The Germans tore the country apart. The Poles don't bother them when they come. But they see a black person and they want to tear off your head."

We found a bar that appeared quiet. Now it was the bartender who did a double take when Ariel spoke to him in Polish. A handful of men seated at the counter glared at us as we took our beer to one of the tables. The room, tinted a harsh blue from the strobe lights, had an eerie quality. We huddled close to one another and spoke in whispers. Omni asked what I'd been doing in Poland. I told her where I'd gone, the sorrow I felt. She nodded. "This country doesn't have any tourism. Jews like you come here because you want to see what happened to your people. But regular tourists don't want to come. There's nothing for them to do here."

I was surprised to hear Omni speak so negatively about Poland. I asked if she was sorry she'd left Cuba. She shook her head. "I've had a lot of opportunities in Poland. I've become known as an artist. I've shared the stage with famous Polish artists. The Poles like to see me perform, because to them I'm exotic."

"So on stage it's okay to be black?"

"On stage, they love it that I'm black," Omni replied. "I'm the sexy mulata."

I asked her what she thought she'd be doing if she were still in Cuba.

"In Cuba, I'd be doing the same thing. Singing. Maybe by now I would've been performing with a big band in Havana. And I'll tell you, I know what they earn and it's shitty. They play an all-night concert and earn five dollars, after performing for thousands of tourists who paid twenty dollars to get in."

She sighed and took a sip of her beer. It had warmed up inside the bar. She slipped off her jacket and rolled up the sleeves of her sweater. Pointing to her forearms, she laughed and said she wasn't getting enough sun in Poland. Her black skin was pale. "It's hard to be here," she added. "But if I were in Cuba right now, I'd be trying to leave. I'd be trying to find work in another country."

SEVEN MONTHS LATER, IN JULY 2007, I returned to Havana. Danayda had expected to be leaving Cuba around then. I had thought I'd document her departure. But when I got there, it was clear she wouldn't be leaving anytime soon. Although she and Carlos had received their passports, their tickets to Israel hadn't arrived. She was exasperated. She wanted to be gone, but she was still in Cuba, waiting.

Danayda was waiting for the day she'd pack her things into a suitcase, like a tourist going on vacation, paint her nails silver, and dab perfume on her wrists.

Danayda was waiting for the day when she'd apply mascara to her lashes and leave a kiss on a handkerchief with her fuchsia lipstick.

Danayda was waiting for the day when she'd go to the airport dressed all in white. A belt, also white, would rest on the hips of her tight white jeans, the front-zippered white sleeveless blouse revealing a bit of cleavage, the pink scarf lined with sequins serving as a headband around her gleaming straightened hair. A little white handbag would hang from a thin strap on her shoulder.

Danayda was waiting for the day when she'd say goodbye to all the neighbors. They'd utter only one word to her in parting: *Triunfa.* Triumph.

Danayda was waiting for the day when she'd ride in the borrowed van, sitting between Carlos and her mother, her tolerant mother, a Jehovah's Witness who let her choose her father's Jewish faith.

Danayda was waiting for the day when, on the way to the airport, the afternoon sunlight would blind her eyes but she'd look ahead unblinking.

Danayda was waiting for the day when, finally at the airport, just before she stepped through the glass door marked "Exit," she'd say goodbye to her mother. She warned her mother not to cry, because if she did, it would make leaving unbearable.

After so much waiting, the ticket arrived four months later, and the day came, November 5, 2007, when Danayda dressed all in white.

I wasn't there, but I asked the photographer Humberto Mayol to take pictures of Danayda's last day in Cuba. She looked radiant, her face shining with hope. She was glad to be making this trip with her husband. At the suggestion of his parents, he'd also dressed in white for the departure—white for a pure heart, white for new beginnings, white for Obatalá, the *orisha* who represents the light of consciousness. Also with Danayda was her father, who at the age of sixty-seven felt too old to be an immigrant. He was leaving Cuba with his third wife and her fifteen-year-old daughter. As if in mourning, Levy and his wife were dressed in black from head to toe.

At the airport their departure was very matter-of-fact, not like the dramatic departures in the 1960s, when I left with my family, when leaving was an act of betrayal against the nation, a form of treason against the Revolution. *Gusanos,* they called us, "worms," and we were strip-searched in case we carried hidden jewels, but also just to humiliate us. Globalization had quieted the revolutionary patriotic fervor, normalized emigration. It was no longer a political act to leave Cuba. No comment was made. No animosity. Suitcases were checked to their final destination, passports stamped *salida definitiva*, definitive departure. A simple *Buen viaje* uttered by the immigration officer, a wish for a good journey.

Nothing remained afterward but to say goodbye, the goodbye both desired and feared. When it came time for Danayda to say goodbye, her mother began crying, and she began crying, and the words she'd wanted to say wouldn't come. Tears blocked her throat, clung to her tongue. She couldn't speak.

Only eighteen and she was leaving.

What did leaving mean, anyway? Danayda had never been on a plane before, never gone anywhere that wasn't Cuba. What lay beyond the ocean? What wider world remained to be discovered? She imagined this unknown world from the images she'd seen in magazines and on television. She imagined it from watching throughout her girlhood the carefree life led by the tourists, Spaniards and Italians, attracted to women of her brown complexion. And the years of watching American Jewish visitors on the humanitarian missions had deeply influenced her. They brought with them a sense of Jewish unity, of being one people, which appealed to her. They had enticed her with the endless supply of things they brought from a part of the world where things never seemed to be lacking, and she longed to be a part of that world herself.

Only eighteen and Danayda was saying goodbye to her country and to a mother who was a Jehovah's Witness and couldn't leave with her. She felt so many different emotions: anger that her country didn't offer her the future she wanted for herself; sorrow that her girlhood was gone for good; fear that she'd made the wrong decision, that it was all a mistake, that she'd never manage life in a new language, in a foreign place. All she could do was step through the door to the other side and not look back. Her mother was weeping. If she turned and saw her mother's tears, she'd lose her nerve. She resisted offering a last wave to her mother. As she boarded the plane, she regretted her actions—she could feel the face of her mother dissolving in her memory, as if seeing her now through a rainy window.

THE FIRST COMMUNICATION I RECEIVED from Danayda was an email sent on November 21, 2007. In Spanish she wrote, "ruth i hadn't written before b/c I didn't have internet and i was writing from some friends' account. let me tell you we are all fine here i finally made my big dream come true."

From my home in Michigan I wrote back and asked Danayda for more details about her apartment. I also asked her what she missed of Cuba. On November 27 she replied, again in Spanish, "ruth let me tell you papi and i are in the same building, four apartments apart, the apartments are very pretty, mine's on the top floor, it has 2 rooms, 1 bath, a little balcony for hanging clothes, a kitchen and a huge dining room. here in the merkaz [absorption center] there are 4 cuban families and we all get along, we help each other with everything. . . . what do i miss. . . . . don't even ask, i miss my rowdy neighbors, potholes in the streets, cuban pizzas, the camellos, everything. but that's normal, good or bad i was born there and you always miss what's yours even if you didn't always like everything about it. i need my mama and miss her very much. you can't imagine how many times i've wanted to shout her name and run out to look for her. but i have to be strong since every immigrant has to go through this. and i knew that our separation was going to be very hard. okay ruth i'll leave you now because i have to make dinner. carlos sends greetings and tomorrow i'll send you my papa's email so you can write to him, he sends you greetings too. chao."

Over the next few months we were in frequent email communication, which we never had while Danayda was in Cuba, because she didn't have a computer and depended, like most Cubans, on a public Internet system that involved waiting in long lines for a couple of precious minutes in cyberspace. Only email messages could be sent and received. Access to the web was blocked by the government.

Danayda was enjoying her new online freedom. She sent greeting cards with "I love you" and "I'm thinking of you" messages to as many as thirty-four recipients at a time. She developed a fondness for messages about needing to hold on to your faith in God even during tough times. One carried the subject line, "It really breaks your heart to see these images." This was a PowerPoint presentation in Spanish showing images of emaciated Holocaust survivors, starving children covered with flies in Africa and India, and a mother holding a dead child, reduced to skin and bones, looking into the camera with accusing eyes. Recipients of this message were reminded to complain less about their troubles and count their blessings.

Danayda took the time to send a poem she chose specifically for me.

The poem was about friendship. It began, "A friend is one who walks by your side during good times and bad times." Another line was "A friend is one who can guess what's worrying you and tries to make you feel better."

I'm not sure why, but I put off calling Danayda. Upon arriving in Israel she bought a cell phone and sent me the number in an email. Still, I hesitated. Maybe I wanted to remain in denial that she wasn't in Cuba anymore. Maybe I didn't want to lose the privilege of watching her live the parallel life I didn't get to live.

IT TOOK ME SEVEN MONTHS TO CALL HER. On a Tuesday in June, I dialed her number on my home phone. I was shocked at how easily I got through. Instead of a ring sound while waiting to be connected, a pleasant male voice sang in Hebrew.

She answered in Spanish. *¿Sí?*

I simply said, *"¿Hola, Danayda?,"* and she immediately recognized my voice and said she was happy to hear from me.

Had I reached her at a bad moment, I asked.

Not at all, she said. She was just getting home from work.

What time was it there? I asked.

Ten o'clock in the evening, she replied.

And you work such late hours?

Yes, she said. She worked from six in the morning until one-thirty in the afternoon and then again from seven until nine-thirty in the evening. Every day except Friday, when she worked until ten-thirty in the morning. Saturdays she didn't work; it was Shabbat. Then on Sunday she went back to work again.

And where do you work? I asked.

It was a building with lots of offices, she said. There were lawyers, dentists, and doctors who did breast implants.

She was ashamed, I could tell. She didn't want to tell me more. But I wanted to know.

What do you do there? I asked.

She paused a moment longer before saying she cleaned the lobby, floors, windows, everything. She didn't mind the work. Previously she'd worked in a factory where people stood over you yelling orders and Russian coworkers left banana peels on the floor so you'd slip and break your neck. She was working ten hours a day, she said, but she was happy to be earning 200 shekels. It wasn't like Cuba, where if you didn't feel like working one day, you just stayed home since you weren't going to earn much anyway. There was no way she was going to miss a day of work and lose 200 shekels.

I switched the phone to speaker mode and looked up the conversion to dollars. She was earning the equivalent of $59.21 a day. It was less than minimum wage in the United States but about six times what most people in Cuba earned in a month.

She was happy, she said, very happy to be in Israel, though initially she'd been upset to hear they were being sent to Beersheva, in the Negev, smack in the middle of the desert. Nothing could be further from the memory of Havana, where the ocean was always within sight and you could feel its moisture on your flesh. At the beginning, she cried all the time and wanted to go back to Cuba. Her father reminded her there was no going back. They'd made a decision and had to live with it. She took pills for her nerves until two months ago. She only took half a pill now and then, if she needed it. She was happy. She was prepared to stay in Beersheva for the rest of her life.

With her first paycheck, she bought a DVD player for her mother and sent it to her by certified mail. Within a week it arrived in Cuba.

Your mother must have been pleased, I said.

Yes, Danayda said, she was thrilled. But the DVD didn't work with her mother's old television. She had to wait until her next paycheck to send money so her mother could buy herself a new television.

How was Carlos? How was her father? I asked.

They were both well, she said. They'd all gotten together on Sunday for a meal. It was her birthday. She had turned nineteen.

I wanted to kick myself. I knew the date of her birthday, but I'd forgotten. My phone call was two days late.

Carlos, she said, was working in a factory where they manufactured bathroom fixtures. He was making sinks, toilet bowls, bathtubs. He worked different shifts each week, morning, midday, and night. When he worked Saturdays, they paid him double. It was hard and he came home tired.

She too arrived tired from work. He had the more grueling job, she felt, so she took care of the household chores. In Cuba she rarely ever cooked. Her mother and mother-in-law were nearby, and Carlos liked to cook. But in Israel she cooked, cleaned, and washed their clothes. They'd moved out of the absorption center into their own apartment. She liked it better, except she had to follow the norms of the Orthodox Jews who lived in the building. Once, she'd thrown a load of clothes into the washing machine on a Saturday. Within minutes the neighbors, who never said hello or good morning, came knocking and scolded her for working on Shabbat.

As for her father, Danayda said he didn't miss Cuba. He didn't expect to return, at least not for a long time. He did miss the Centro Sefaradí, though. He had trouble finding a synagogue where he felt at home. He started attending a Moroccan synagogue and liked it; they chanted in the Sephardic style, so it sounded more like Cuba. He was still living in the absorption center with his wife and stepdaughter. He was given a pension, but it was modest. He wanted to work. The problem was no one wanted to employ a sixty-seven-year-old male immigrant, even one who knew several languages and had directed a synagogue for fifteen years. All he'd managed to find was the occasional job sweeping a staircase or a hallway.

DANAYDA TOLD ME THAT OMNI WANTED TO hear from me and that I should call her. After we hung up, I googled Omni, and her name came up right away. I found some YouTube videos of her recent performances, including a New Year's Eve concert in Krakow's market square. She was still singing salsa but had added rap to her repertoire and had formed an all-women band with Polish musicians. On her website she called herself a *mulata con sabor,* a mulata with flavor.

I couldn't get through to Omni by phone, so I sent her an email. She wrote back right away and suggested we Skype. A moment later we were connected. I told Omni I'd just spoken to Danayda. She told me that they spoke almost every day via Skype. In the past few months they'd spoken more than in the past six years since she'd left Cuba. Using the cameras on their computers, they could see each other when they talked.

Omni wanted to know what Danayda had told me.

I repeated what Danayda had said—that she wanted to spend the rest of her life in Beersheva.

She's lying to you, Omni replied. Danayda had told her that she was miserable and wanted to leave and go to Canada or come to Poland and perform in her salsa group. She complained that things were too expensive in Israel and that you had to work much too hard to make money. Omni told her things were expensive everywhere, and that, wherever you went, you had to work hard to make money. Life wasn't going to be easier someplace else.

I mentioned that Danayda, at the age of nineteen, had taken on a lot of responsibility.

Omni thought her sister was still immature, still a *muchachita.* She hadn't hesitated to tell Danayda that she needed to diet and trim her mermaid curves if she wanted to perform with the salsa group. In Cuba they consider women beautiful if they're full-bodied, if they've got *ma-sita*, if they're built like Jennifer Lopez and have big *nalgas*. In Europe, she warned her sister, it was skinny women who were attractive.

Do you watch your own weight? I asked Omni.

Yes, of course, she replied. She was the leader of the salsa group and constantly watched what she ate so as not to put on a single pound.

Omni sounded annoyed that Danayda had followed in her path and also left Cuba. She spoke with an older sister's concern and exasperation, and maybe a touch of guilt. What need did Danayda have to leave? She wasn't lacking anything. Her father gave her whatever she wanted—she had clothes, she ate steak. Still, she started saying, I'm leaving, I'm leaving. Maybe because that's what everyone says in Cuba. Now she's crying that she misses her *mamá*. She's so smart and she's cleaning floors, doing the scut work. She's having a harder time in Israel than she ever had in Cuba. She wears those scarves in her hair, and they think she's an Arab and they watch her like a hawk when she goes shopping. She has to wait until they deposit her salary in her account and all she eats is bread until the money arrives. She says she doesn't want to stay there, but I tell her, No, you wanted to leave Cuba. This is how it is.

WHEN I CALLED DANAYDA A FEW DAYS LATER, it was seven in the evening on Saturday and she and Carlos were on their way to Hebrew classes with a private teacher. I agreed to call back. On her return, she explained why they had hired their own teacher. Beersheva was full of Russian immigrants. There were also Ethiopians and Bedouins and Arabs. And people from all over Latin America—from Peru, Uruguay, Colombia, and Argentina. But the Russians had started arriving in the early 1990s, after the fall of the Soviet Union, and they continued to come. According to Danayda, they ran the town and they made anyone who wasn't Russian feel like a cockroach. The teachers in the state-run Hebrew *ulpan* classes were all Russians, and when they taught Hebrew they explained things in Russian. Even their Hebrew sounded like Russian. She and Carlos had found it impossible to learn in the *ulpan*. Now with their Argentine teacher explaining things to them in Spanish, they were making rapid progress learning Hebrew. Still, there were times when she couldn't get her tongue to form a single Hebrew word. Just the other day she'd not been able to stop weeping when her boss told her to clean an ashtray she'd already cleaned and someone dirtied a moment later.

Crying was something she did a lot of in Israel.

She had fulfilled her biggest dream, which was to visit the Wailing Wall in Jerusalem. When she got there and wanted to offer a prayer of thanks to God, all she could do was weep. She no longer knew what language to speak.

I asked Danayda if she'd thought of leaving Israel and going to Poland to live with her sister. She sounded surprised. To visit, certainly, she said, just like she'd enjoy traveling to Michigan to see me. That was the main reason she'd left Cuba, so she could go wherever she wanted. She had attained the freedom she'd longed for: the freedom to travel anywhere in the world. Of course, first she needed to make money. But she intended to stay in Israel.

Have you experienced racism in Israel?

She laughed. All the time, she said. On the bus, the Russians stare at her, but she learned to stare back. On Saturday, after Shabbat ended, she liked to wear a long skirt and a scarf in her hair and go window-shopping at the mall. The guards inspect her from head to toe. Cubana, she tells them. They keep looking at her suspiciously. Maybe it's because she can't afford to buy anything in all the pretty stores. It will be another two or three years, she thinks. Right now she buys clothes and scarves in the Arab market, in the *shuk*. The Arab men flirt with her, as do the Bedouins. The Ethiopians have mistaken her for one of their own. But she takes it all with a dose of humor. She says she tells them, "Am I that black? I just have a little bit of color."

Being in Israel wasn't easy, Danayda admitted. She'd hoped to get better work. Hoped to do manicures and style hair, the kind of work she enjoyed doing in Cuba. And Carlos had hoped to work as a cook; they'd turned him down at restaurants because they were kosher and Carlos wasn't Jewish.

They had to take whatever work was available. No job was too humble, Danayda said. She worked to send things to her mother; she worked to one day bring her mother to live with her in Israel. She and Carlos were saving up for a trip back to Cuba. She was waiting. Waiting again. Waiting to be on a beach in Cuba. Any beach. Even the worst beach in Cuba would be good enough.

I CALLED THE FOLLOWING FRIDAY. As I listened to the Hebrew tune in the moments before I was connected to Danayda, I thought about how I was becoming an armchair anthropologist. In the past, to talk to Danayda I had to go to Cuba. Now I could sit at home and take notes as we spoke long distance.

Calling this time, I'd woken Danayda. It was ten o'clock in the evening in Israel. I apologized. She said it was okay. Carlos was sound asleep. She moved to another room so we could talk. I apologized again. She said I really shouldn't worry. They often stayed up late on Friday. But they'd both come home exhausted. They showered, ate, and went straight to bed. She had been waiting the entire week for it to be Friday, just so she could sleep. All she wanted was to sleep. They didn't sleep much during the week. She wanted Saturdays not to end, and for Sunday not to arrive too soon.

What other questions did I have for her?

Having woken her up, I knew it wasn't the best time to spring a question about Israeli-Palestinian relations. How's the political situation there now? I ventured. Are things quiet?

Beersheva was calm, Danayda said. She was looking out the window and there wasn't a soul in the street. On the news she'd heard Hamas announce that their next big attack would be in Beersheva. Shortly before they'd arrived from Cuba, a suicide bomber on a Beersheva bus had detonated himself and everyone riding on the bus had been killed.

Are you worried?

There is violence everywhere in the world, she replied. In Cuba on any street corner they could hack you with a machete. Anywhere at all you could be struck down.

I felt bad stealing her sleep. I said goodbye and asked if she'd have trouble falling asleep again. Not at all, she assured me. As soon as she put her head on the pillow she'd be asleep.

Before leaving Cuba, Danayda had told her mother she could never have given her life for Cuba, but she was prepared to give her life for Israel. I hoped she'd never have to.

I WASN'T SATISFIED BEING AN ARMCHAIR anthropologist. When an invitation to speak at the University of Beersheva came along in October 2009, I eagerly agreed to go and give three lectures, just so I could talk to Danayda and Levy in person.

They came to see me the same night I arrived. Levy had lost a lot of weight. Danayda had put on a lot of weight. In the span of two years in Israel, their lives had been turned upside down. Levy and his third wife had parted ways, and she'd left for Spain with her daughter. He told me he was never a nostalgic person, but he now spent all his free time searching on his computer for Cuban *boleros*, love songs. He didn't have a computer in Cuba. In Israel, upon arriving, he'd been given a hand-me-down. Danayda and Carlos had also split up. He'd moved to Tel Aviv and was working at an auto repair shop where they employed Latin American immigrants. Danayda's boyfriend was Israeli, a son of Rumanian immigrants. He was tall, bulky, and glum.

Danayda and Levy had made a concerted effort to become fluent in

Hebrew and communicated easily with Israelis. Their one major disappointment was how difficult it was to obtain dignified work. Danayda told me she'd cleaned more floors in Israel in two years than she'd cleaned in Cuba in eighteen. She was working in a peanut factory to make enough money to pay her cell phone bill. I wanted to film her in the factory and tried to seek permission, but I wasn't allowed to even enter. Just being outside the factory, surrounded by the peanut dust and debris, I imagined the horrid conditions inside.

In hopes of becoming a hairdresser, Danayda had enrolled in a beauty school. Her teacher was a gay Israeli man and the other students were veiled Bedouin women. The teacher had convinced the Bedouin women to remove their veils so they could style one another's hair. They resisted at first. The teacher reminded them he was gay and had no interest in them as women. Finally they agreed, covering up again afterward. Danayda herself had taken to wearing long skirts and scarves in her hair—to become Dvorah, as she now called herself, a woman she could never be in Cuba.

On my last day in Beersheva, a Friday afternoon, we waited for Levy to finish sweeping stairways and for Danayda's boyfriend to come home from his job as a security guard. We'd decided to go on a little excursion to the Dead Sea.

Once at the beach, Levy and Danayda's boyfriend refused to remove their street clothes, even though they had their bathing suits on underneath. Neither wanted to go into the water. Danayda and I stripped down to our swimsuits and got in.

The Dead Sea felt like nothing I'd ever felt before. Heavy water. Salty water. Silky water. I couldn't advance because of the rocks on the sea bottom.

"Come on!" Danayda called to me.

"It hurts! The rocks are scratching my feet," I replied.

"They're not rocks," Danayda said. "That's salt. It's all salt."

I bent down and scooped up beautiful necklaces of salt crystals.

Danayda took my hand. Together we waded in deeper, stopping when we could no longer touch bottom. Then we relaxed. Let our bodies float. I imagined us held aloft by the tears shed by the world's exiles and refugees.

Of course I thought about Lot's wife in the Old Testament, famous for looking back, despite being warned not to, and how she turned into a pillar of salt.

I was a pillar of salt that afternoon at the Dead Sea. Since she's determined only to look ahead, I looked back for Danayda, thinking of the soft warm ocean she left in Cuba.

THAT DAY I DIDN'T YET KNOW HOW IT would feel to return to Cuba and no longer find Danayda there, this girl whom I'd watched grow up, watched as the teddy bear placed in her hands led her to imagine a new life in another place, far away.

A few months later, I was walking through Havana's Chinatown with my Michigan students. Our semester abroad program had just begun. Everything about Cuba struck them as fascinating, and everything seemed just spooky enough that they liked me to lead them by the hand. I was walking in front, showing them around my native city like a hen with her little chicks in tow.

We stopped at a traffic light and I wanted to turn and say, You know, there's a young woman who lived a few blocks from here. Her name is Danayda. She now calls herself Dvorah. She used to walk on these streets we're walking on now. But she's not here anymore. I can't come see her in Cuba. She left, just like I left when I was a child. I miss her. It makes me wonder why I still come back.

I didn't want to make my students sad. After all, I'd brought them to Cuba for a fun-filled learning experience in one of the most beautiful islands of the Caribbean.

"Goodbye, Danayda," I whispered softly, so no one heard me. Not that it really mattered. Danayda was long gone. Long gone.

DANAYDA'S STORY CONTINUES TO UNFOLD. Tired of doing menial work in Israel, she went to Spain for seven months to sell Dead Sea bath products and cosmetics for an Israeli company. Her Israeli boyfriend broke up with her for leaving Israel. Then in Spain she met another young man, Junior, a car salesman from the Dominican Republic. They fell in love. On her return to Israel, they communicated via video chat and Facebook, until she joined him in the Dominican Republic. On YouTube there is an endearing video of her arrival at the airport in Santo Domingo and she and Junior falling into each other's arms and kissing passionately.

Now she goes by the name Deby and she's happy that she's found love. Junior is a good young man, she says, *un buen muchacho*. He's promised to set her up with a beauty parlor, or better, a nail salon, because his sister already has a beauty parlor. He's aware of Danayda's Jewish heritage and has asked her to teach him Hebrew. He put up a mezuzah at the threshold of their house, as is customary among Jews. The neighbors, never having heard of a mezuzah, joked that he was installing a special alarm system to protect Danayda while he was away at work. Junior has completely given up pork, Danayda tells me, even though she admits she finds it mouth-watering, seeing it for sale on every street corner in Santo Domingo. But every time she wants to succumb to the temptation, he tells her, "No, Deby, we can't eat that." On Facebook there are pictures of them looking amorous on a Dominican beach. He seems thoroughly enchanted with the fullness of her curvy body.

His family has been welcoming. His mother, an evangelical Christian, visits every afternoon while Danayda waits for Junior to come home from work. Junior's mother reminds Danayda of her own mother. They watch soap operas and sometimes they'll go to his mother's church. "Don't even try to convert me," she tells the evangelicals. "I come from Israel."

A synagogue stood on every block in Israel. There's only one synagogue for the entire D.R. It's located two hours from where she lives. One day she'll go, she says. Of course, she'll go.

Talking on the phone from Michigan, I ask Danayda how she likes the D.R. She says it's like Cuba, but with better living conditions. Almost. Blackouts do seem to happen almost every night.

She's in Sabana Perdida, I learn. I look it up online and discover it's the poorest part of Santo Domingo.

But her mother is glad Danayda is no longer in Israel; she was constantly worried Danayda would be hurt in a terrorist attack.

Cuba is so close, and Danayda wishes she could bring her mother to the D.R. for a visit. She and Junior just don't have enough money at the moment. Paying for their wedding and getting her papers straightened out has used up their savings—really Junior's savings, since at this point she has nothing and is depending on him.

I ask if she's nostalgic for Cuba. Yes, she says. She can't help crying when she's online and sees the videos that tourists have uploaded of Havana's Chinatown or the Malecón or the Coppelia outdoor ice-cream shop. But go back to live there? Never, she says, never. She has no hope things will improve. Of course, only God knows for sure.

And Israel? I ask, do you miss Israel?

Yes, she misses Israel. But she misses her father most of all. He chose to stay there alone, her father who left Cuba for her sake.

Did you bring anything with you from Israel? I ask.

My prayer book, she replies.

Every Friday she puts on a long skirt, covers her head, and sometimes she lights the candles. She prays—by herself. Prays in Hebrew "to Adonai *y mi gente*," she says, to God and her people.

As we begin saying goodbye, I'm left with a melancholy image of

Danayda: twenty-two years old, a lone Jew in the tropics, a Robinson Crusoe clutching at the Jewish identity her father nurtured in her from the time she was a little girl holding a teddy bear. She'd planned to stay in Israel forever. Planned to be at her father's side. Planned to keep working to support her mother in Cuba and bring her to Israel. But a good man from the Caribbean won her heart. She believes in love, believes in romance. Perhaps after four years of hard work in Israel, she realized that as an Afro-Cuban woman she was always going to struggle to fit in. She'd be seen as an Arab before being seen as a Jew. It was a matter of color, and in the D.R. her color is the right color. And people are friendly in the easygoing way people are in Cuba; they smile, they greet you in the street. She feels comfortable. But Israel remains a part of her. In Sabana Perdida she stubbornly asserts her Jewishness, asserts it out of context.

Before we hang up, she tells me she wants to see *Adio Kerida* again, to see herself as a girl in Cuba. She'd like to show the movie to Junior and his family. I offer to send her a copy and ask her for her address. She gives me Junior's full name and then she asks him for the address. He'd been sitting next to her as we talked on the phone. As she repeats the address to me word by word, it shocks me to think that she has no idea where she's been living for the past two months. It seems that for the moment she's chosen to surrender her will—putting her faith in a good man who'll take care of her. She's waiting again. Waiting for the future to arrive.

Departure had been her goal—not to be in Cuba anymore. She journeyed far, all the way to the Middle East, with a stop in Spain, only to come back to the Caribbean, to the island next door to the one she abandoned. She gained the freedom to travel anywhere in the world. But the world was bigger than she imagined. And so she chose to come partway home.

Danayda married Junior and posted pictures of herself on Facebook, in a white wedding gown and, soon after, in a maternity blouse, pressing her hands against her belly. Later she uploaded a *National Geographic* video clip of a woman giving birth and wrote with exhilaration that she was feeling the baby's first kicks.

I feel I'm stalking her on Facebook as I look over her shoulder to see what news she feels is worth posting about her life. As this writing goes to press, I need to add another installment: it is 2 AM on August 6, 2012, and I've learned via Facebook that Danayda has just given birth to a daughter, Nahomi Bethel. Family and friends have sent congratulations and filled her corner of cyberspace with praise for her newborn little girl—*es una muñequita*; she's a little doll, someone wrote. Belatedly, as usual, I add my own congratulations to the end of the list.

I can still picture Danayda holding that teddy bear in Havana—the first temptation from the "outside world" to reach her, to seduce her into leaving home. Now she's a mother, and, not being in Cuba anymore, she'll be able to get a teddy bear for her own child. No need for charity.

Was that the point of her journey, in the end?

It's not up to me to judge. I'm only the anthropologist in her life.

I do know I'll always call my young friend by her Cuban name, Danayda, the name she left behind on the island that belongs to us both.

I do know I'll keep telling her story as long as she lets me, as long as she tolerates my being the archivist of her hopes and dreams, her memory-keeper, the one who stood by, biting her tongue, as she decided the only future was somewhere else.

How I wish I had more to give Danayda.

All I can offer her, with any certainty, is the witness of my eyes.

*cristy always prays
for my safe return*

....

After being "poked" by several people, some of them family, some of them friends I knew well, and others whom I didn't know at all, I decided to join Facebook. Wary of the whole process, I feared that Facebook would steal as much of my time as email, so I posted only a basic profile. Soon I had a hundred friends, then two hundred. I quickly came to understand the seduction of Facebook. Late one evening, catching myself spending hours reading the profiles of my friends and the postings on their walls, I realized how easy it is to get caught up in the minutiae of everyone's rambling thoughts and relentless activities. I vowed to keep my Facebook presence to a minimum.

Cristy was one of the people who'd "poked" me, more than once. Now that I'm on Facebook, she sends me messages constantly. Her messages come in batches, like notes in a bottle tossed into the sea and flung ashore like flotsam. She communicates furiously when she's able to get online, which isn't easy in Cuba. For my birthday, she sent me a picture of a rose as a gift. She also sent me a "Sexy Men" photo, which I haven't yet looked at. She sends me requests to reply to quizzes—"Which angel are you?" or "*¿Eres positiva o pesimista?*" I've not yet gotten around to answering them. She's asked me three times to be a Facebook "relative" even though we aren't kin; not knowing whether to confirm, I've not responded.

When we were little girls, Cristy and I were neighbors. I'm just a couple of years older than she. We lived in an apartment across the hall, a mirror image of the apartment where Cristy lived with her parents, Consuelito and Edilberto. Her parents chose to stay after the Revolution because Edilberto was a revolutionary. Mami told me that before we left Cuba she and Papi made a pretense of telling Edilberto we were going on vacation and would soon return.

For Cristy, being able to communicate on Facebook is a lifeline. Being in Cuba, she feels shipwrecked. She shares the old two-bedroom apartment in the no longer posh but still leafy Vedado neighborhood of Havana with her husband, Pepe, their thirty-year-old daughter, Monica, and her parents. For Cristy, this fifth-floor walk-up is the only home she knows. She's never lived anywhere else. The family also has a separate apartment on the ground floor that belonged to her mother's two spinster aunts. After their deaths, Cristy acquired the apartment and turned it into a rental, which supports the whole family. "We eat thanks to that apartment," she likes to say. It has new beds, a new stove, a new fridge, new curtains, and air-conditioning, luxuries that Cristy and her family make available to tourists but not for themselves.

Each time I travel to Cuba, I stop and visit Cristy and her family. Cristy speaks openly to me about her life and her disappointments. She suffers from acne and I come bearing the Neutrogena soaps she requests, which are unavailable in Cuba. I bring news from the rest of the world and a glimpse of the latest fashions in the clothes and shoes I wear, but I don't try to compete with Cristy's sexy attire. She favors short shorts or a clingy turquoise minidress and four-inch platform sandals. She proudly flaunts her cellulite.

With dizzying speed I come and go, disappearing and reappearing like a magic act. Since my time in Cuba is brief, I'm always in a rush. Cristy tries to get me to slow down, sit around, do nothing, but I never can. In their household, Consuelito and Pepe do all the cooking, and they prepare delicious meals for me—simple things, like beans and rice, tomato salad, fried plantains, and slices of mango, which I love, but which Cristy has come to find boring. I eat in a hurry, Cristy eyeing me with affection and longing. I'm the woman she might have become if her parents had made a different decision after Fidel Castro took power. With her parents in the room, Cristy is in the habit of announcing, "You're lucky, Ruti—your parents saved you, they took you out of here. Not like me—my parents kept me here so I could suffer."

Cristy likes to say she'd go anywhere in the world just to be able to leave Cuba. "But I can't leave the *viejos* behind," she's quick to add, referring to her parents. "So I'm stuck here." She's applied for the *bombo*, the American immigration lottery. Yet for all the frustration she feels about her diminished opportunities, I know Cristy adores her parents and forgives them for having chosen to stay in Cuba. Rubbing shoulders with Mimi and Pipo every single day, being able to scold Monica for staying up late, that is the only life she truly considers worth living.

Unable to experience what it might be like to live elsewhere, Cristy spends her free time online. She uses a borrowed Internet connection that allows her broad access, more than most people have in a country where the web is controlled by the government. Being on Facebook is how she vicariously goes places and stays connected with friends like me, who claim they're Cuban but don't live on the island anymore.

So there I am, in November 2008, crafting my first Evite on Facebook for a book presentation at the Miami Book Fair. I'm nervous about whom to send it to: only those who might actually be able to attend the event? Or all my Facebook friends? I notice that people send Evites to everyone. Obviously, Cristy can't come to the Miami Book Fair. Would it be cruel to send it to her, then? But it also doesn't feel right to exclude her. The Evite, I decide, will be a way of letting Cristy know I've published a new book, an anthology about the Cuban diaspora, which sets forth the concept that Cuba is "a portable island."

In Cuba people are always dreaming of other places. Blame it on the fact that the arrival of the revolutionary paradise has been perpetually postponed. Blame it on the underdevelopment and neocolonialism that plagues all the countries of the Caribbean. Blame it on something more primordial, that when living on an island your eyes tend to fog up with visions of lands beyond the sea. Especially since 1959 Cubans have become an intensely diasporic people. We live everywhere, from Argentina to Australia. Now that 20 percent of the Cuban people reside outside the country, we're a people of many floating islands, a people who travel incessantly, a people always seeking and never quite finding home. Cubans are some of the world's greatest experts at saying goodbye. But there's still the 80 percent who know only too well where home is, and they wave at those who leave and welcome back those who return.

Cristy, who's never been on a plane, knows all about my fear of plane crashes. "Don't worry, Ruti, you'll be fine. I'll be praying to the Virgin of La Caridad del Cobre for you, so you'll arrive safely."

I'm glad Cristy prays for me. I'm sure her prayers help.

For Cristy, the island isn't portable. Home is the same apartment where she's lived since she was born, the mirror image of the one I might still be living in across the hall. Her island is nailed to the sea.

I guess I shouldn't be surprised that Cristy is the first to respond to my Evite. She checks off the box saying she'll attend. She posts a note saying she'll be waiting for me in Miami. She plans to arrive early, she says, and I imagine her melancholy smile.

I KNOW BETTER THAN TO TELL CRISTY how often I travel, how often I'm away from home, if home is Michigan, where I'm employed by a university so large I know only a handful of my colleagues, and where I own a house painted in tropical colors, sea greens and turquoise blues that cheer me when it's snowing. Cristy would find it sad that I don't see my parents every day; sad I don't see Gabriel, now an adult, every day; sad that I move around in the world like an orphan.

I'm a well-heeled orphan. I travel 50,000 miles a year. I'm Gold Medallion. I scramble to get on the plane, together with the other privileged travelers. I go to Europe. I go to Latin America. I travel to California. To Miami whenever I can—now that I'm older I appreciate an ocean that's as warm as soup. I lost Cuba as a little girl. But I've gained an entire life up in the air, a life going to other places, a life spent between places.

However much I long for the island I once called home, I'm not beholden to any one place. I'm not stuck anywhere. But I'm also never sure whether I belong anywhere.

"¿Qué se te perdió en Cuba?" Baba asked every time I stopped to see her in Miami Beach on my way to Havana. What did I lose in Cuba? She wanted me to forget Cuba, move on.

But I didn't listen. Whatever I lost in Cuba, I'd find it. So many return trips. I felt as if Cuba was mine again. I was part of a group of Cuban American scholars, artists, and writers who went to the island when no one else from the United States did. We were brave. We were naïve. We were convinced that if only Cubans talked to other Cubans, we'd make the island whole again. We tried to believe our American identity was insignificant, a mask. We wanted to strip down to our Cuban selves. We offered promises of reconciliation. We dreamed of building a bridge with our common culture, memory, and language.

Fluffy stuff.

Then the big guns came, guys and gals with money, connections, and the power to make others listen and take notice. *Volvieron los americanos.* The real Americans returned. Ry Cooder arrived and reinvented the Buena Vista Social Club. Curators from MoMA came and loaded their suitcases with art to carry off to Fifth Avenue. Photographers found the ruins of Havana as mesmerizing as those of Pompeii. They marketed an image of the alluring haunted city. Students dove in and grabbed the hot topics: sex tourism and Santería. Medical missions brought aspirin to eradicate the headaches of the born and the unborn. Religious missions brought Bibles and Nike T-shirts. American Jewish missions, an endless stream, came to tell the handful of Cuban Jews they weren't alone; from now on they'd never lack for matzo, abundant bread of affliction, until kingdom come.

I watched them all arrive, my fellow Americans, and fall in love with Cuba. It was the Song of Songs and the bride was my island. She was dressed in finery now. Silk and pearls and diamonds. Things I couldn't afford to give her.

With so many louder voices claiming Cuba, celebrating Cuba, I fell silent. I grew small. Insignificant.

I was again the little girl being led by the hand out of Cuba and urged not to cry.

IN THE COLLEGE TOWN IN MICHIGAN WHERE I live, there are many Americans whom I call "Cuba addicts" because of their need to be continually immersed in Cuban life by traveling to the island and getting their fix. These people also stay on top of all the latest news concerning Cuba, which they happily forward to you in daily email messages. They're passionately concerned that Cuba's uniqueness will be smothered in the near future, "once things change." An "addict" who agreed to be interviewed put it this way: "One of the most powerful things about Cuba is to be away from the things I don't like about the U.S. You can go to Bali or Thailand and still see a McDonald's on the corner. Visually there's something so gratifying about not seeing anything that represents the commercialization of our world. That the U.S. is not there is a huge relief."

I have a friend in town, one of the "Cuba addicts," who likes to quote Joseph Hergesheimer, a forgotten writer on whom Cuba made a lasting impression. In 1920 Hergesheimer wrote, "There are certain cities, strange to the first view, nearer the heart than home." My friend says those words reflect exactly how he feels about Cuba. He made twenty-two visits to the island before marrying a Cuban woman—though, curiously, their initial encounter was through an Internet website. Eventually he was able to bring his wife to Michigan and, soon after, she gave birth to their baby girl. "Now I'm really committed," he says. "I have family down there. I'm married to a Cuban."

What can I say? Who now has a stronger claim to Cuba: I who left the island as a child and no longer have family in Cuba, or my friend, a Michigan native, still unable to speak Spanish, who now has family "down there"? If an identity, like a library book, has an expiration date, mine is surely past due, and the fine for clinging to it can only get heftier.

As Elizabeth Bishop advised, "Practice losing farther, losing faster: places and names, and where it was you meant to travel."

I keep trying.

IT'S BEEN SEVERAL DAYS SINCE I'VE HEARD from Cristy. I miss her messages. So long as she writes to me, so long as we're bound together because of our once having been neighbors as little girls, I can hope I haven't lost Cuba altogether. The other night, feeling low on willpower, I logged onto Facebook. I realized I'd forgotten to congratulate Cristy on her birthday. I was three weeks late. I sent her a message and apologized for being so bad at keeping up with dates. I still don't know how to send pictures of roses and "Sexy Men," so my message lacked the fanfare of those she sends me. I'm thinking I ought to accept her invitation to be a Facebook "relative." Then will I too be able to claim I have family "down there"?

In our cyber reality, where everything is possible and the constraints of time and space and embargoes and an ocean border don't apply, Cristy arrived "early" for my book presentation in Miami.

And I arrived at her birthday party after the candles had burned out.

an old little girl

....

At the last minute I found out about the trip and begged for a spot. "I have to go, please!" I declared. "I was born there!" Although they'd stopped accepting applications, the organizers agreed to make an exception and let me come along. It was 1979, the first time I would return to Cuba. I was joining a group of professors and fellow students from Princeton going on an official university visit.

Winter had arrived. I felt the cold in my bones, but I went running off to Nassau Street to look for something suitably tropical to wear. Hanging from a sale rack in the corner of a store serviced by a snobby saleswoman was the perfect garment: a marked-down white halter dress. The skirt was puffy and I had to wear it without a bra, which was fine back then; I was twenty-two and I could pull off the iconic Marilyn Monroe billowing dress.

In my second year of graduate school in anthropology, I dreamed of returning to my native land to do my dissertation research. Negotiations were under way with the Carter administration to end the embargo against Cuba. After twenty years of broken relations between the United States and Cuba, there was hope of reconciliation.

But the Cuban government was still apprehensive about the threat of capitalist influence and was letting Americans visit for only a week at a time. Our group wasn't permitted to venture beyond Havana unescorted. We stayed at the famed Hotel Nacional, once home to celebrities like Frank Sinatra. On a bluff overlooking the seaside avenue of the Malecón, the hotel exuded faded glamour. On closer inspection, you saw how rundown it was. The air-conditioning was out of order. There were no toilet seats. The bedspreads were ragged. Not that we spent any time in our rooms. Each day we were shepherded around by bus to hear lectures on the triumphs of the Revolution. Our one excursion outside of Havana was to a model farm. A robust woman in army fatigues told us about advances in agriculture. As a reward for listening to her, we were served *guarapo*, sugarcane juice.

I was one of two students of Cuban heritage. When we landed in Havana, a polite man in a white *guayabera* shirtdress awaited us as if we were old friends. He helped me and the other student with our bags and seemed delighted to see us. He sat next to the two of us on the bus during our trips. He asked us repeatedly how we felt about the Revolution and was extremely interested in our replies. He was an informer for the Cuban government, though I didn't know it then. Anyone who'd left Cuba, even as a small child, was a potential security threat and required surveillance. I wish I remembered those interrogations, what I was asked and what I said. Perhaps one day the files of the Ministry of the Interior will be made public and I'll be able to find a report of my statements.

At the time, I must confess, I worried more about being abducted if I wandered a few blocks from the hotel. I wore my white halter dress only once on that first visit back to Havana, because men on the street yelled obscenities, hissed, smacked their lips, whistled, followed me, drew close, and attempted to touch me. Never had I felt so attractive. Never had I felt how dangerous it was to be a young woman. I wanted to cloak myself in a nun's habit, not to feel naked in the street.

One day I snuck away from the official activities and took a taxi to visit Caro, my old nanny. I wasn't sure she'd remember me or even let me into her home. But Mami urged me to seek her out. They'd written letters to one another after we left Cuba, and my mother had kept all the ones she'd received from Caro. "You can trust her with your life," Mami had said of her.

And my mother was right. Caro's integrity shone through in her simplest actions. She knew who I was the minute she saw me. She had pictures of my entire family, kept in the same shoebox where she kept the pictures of her own children. She remembered vividly the little girl I'd been in Cuba. It amused her to recall how feisty I was then. She laughed as she told me about the time she'd accidentally scratched my leg while scrubbing me with a washcloth in the tub. *"Pobrecita,"* poor thing, she'd said to me by way of apology, and I'd told her, "Don't call me *pobrecita*, I'm not *pobrecita*." Caro gave me such a loving welcome that when it was time to leave and she asked when I'd be back, I said, "Soon, very soon." And I meant it.

But those plans fell through before I could even schedule a return trip. A year later, in 1980, relations between Cuba and the United States once more soured. The crisis of the Mariel exodus, leading to the departure of over 120,000 Cubans disaffected with the Revolution, brought about another political rift. Seeking to turn this embarrassing situation to his favor, Fidel Castro forced criminals and mentally ill people, as well as gay men, released from Cuban jails and asylums, to accompany legitimate immigrants on boats heading to Florida. Discarding those he called the "scum of the Revolution," Castro regained ideological control.

The door to the island closed. My first return to Cuba ended in another farewell.

UNABLE TO TRAVEL TO CUBA, I SPENT the next twelve years going back and forth to Spain and Mexico, living as an anthropologist in those adopted homelands.

Then in 1991, as Cuba struggled to avert an economic and moral crisis following the collapse of the Soviet Union, the island opened up again to tourists and Cuban Americans. But legal restrictions still made it difficult to travel on your own, so I signed up with a study group in New York for a one-week visit and asked David to accompany me. By then I'd become a mother and wanted to bring along Gabriel, who was four, but children weren't permitted to travel with the group. Saying goodbye to Gabriel as my parents buckled him into his car seat, I felt as though I were abandoning him. Mami and Papi warned me that I might be trapped in Cuba and never see my child again.

Upon arrival in Cuba, I was besieged by panic attacks. My first trip back had felt like a hazy dream, but the second was a nightmare. I missed Gabriel and kept thinking that he was the same age I'd been when we left Cuba. As I walked with David along the Malecón, my head spun, my legs felt too weak to sustain me. To steady myself, I clutched David's hand. I was as wobbly as a top. Gentle ocean breezes could knock me down. Everything made me cry.

Yet I relished being in a place where people let the sweetest endearments roll off their tongues, calling each other *mi amor* (my love) or *mi cielo* (my sky). When I announced sadly that I'd left as a child and doubted I could still claim a Cuban identity, my new friends in Cuba told me the island was mine. I hadn't lost it. Being born in Cuba I'd forever be Cuban.

So I returned. And returned. And returned. I'd always gone to Spain and Mexico with David, and later with Gabriel too when he was a small child. Now I became a solitary traveler, an obsessive traveler. Gradually the panic attacks subsided. I could stand on my own two feet. Throughout the 1990s and then during the first decade of the new century, I went so frequently to Cuba I barely had time to unpack my bags before it was time to go again.

At first, it was nostalgia that drew me back. My nostalgia was inherited, since I barely remembered Cuba, but that didn't make it any less intense. In the old family photographs that my mother had packed when we left, I saw the little Cuban girl I'd been. I wanted to stand in the same places where I stood as a child: in front of the Patronato Synagogue; on the balcony of our old Vedado apartment; under the thatched gazebo in the Victor Hugo Park amid the banyan trees. Eventually these romantic yearnings gave way to projects I could justify as schoolwork, intellectual pursuits that I could list on my annual report of activities done in the name of my university. I sought bridges between Cuban writers, scholars, and artists on and off the island; I wrote poetry inspired by the discovery of the work of Dulce María Loynaz; and I studied the tiny Jewish community that might have been mine had we stayed. I became a "professional Cuban," building a career out of my search for my roots.

These visits to Cuba lasted a week or two before I'd quickly head back to Michigan. Always glad to have gone back, I was also always relieved to have been able to get out. I was an immigrant at heart. Grateful as I was to have reclaimed Cuba, I knew that the mobility I took for granted in the United States wasn't something I could give up. I'd watched my Cuban artist and writer friends suffer through a wrenching bureaucracy to obtain permission to travel abroad. And much as I enjoyed listening to the musical clatter of Havana's unending street noise, inhaling the lush smells of cigars and sea salt, and joining in the boisterous laughter of my fellow Cubans, I had to admit that when it was over, I welcomed the quiet of my Victorian house in Michigan.

While in Cuba, I didn't doubt I was being observed. Nothing sinister ever occurred, but I still worried. Crowds terrify me, and on those occasions when I happened to be in Cuba during a patriotic holiday, whether May Day or July 26, commemorating the start of the Revolution, I avoided the mass rallies and sat indoors reading a book. Was this improper conduct of mine being noted down somewhere by someone? I felt myself balanced on a tightrope. Would a day come when they'd charge me for a Kafkaesque crime I didn't know I'd committed? And what if Fidel Castro died while I was there? What would happen then?

Slipping back into the cocoon of family life with David and Gabriel, I savored the comforting routines of mealtimes and bedtimes that gave me a sense of security and peace, until I felt again the longing for the thrill of the emotional roller coaster of being in Cuba, where inchoate fear and uncertainty were always mixed with loving welcomes and the heightened sense of being somehow more alive, every moment charged with edgy intensity. In Cuba life was like jazz: improvised. It was the only place in the world where I woke up with a set of plans and found myself doing the most unexpected things. I'd visit a friend for lunch, and when it was time to go, rather than take a taxi, I'd end up on the back of a neighbor's motorcycle, holding on for dear life as we sped through the streets of Havana.

Twenty years passed. As the popular song goes, *Veinte años no es nada.* Twenty years is nothing. But twenty years is *twenty years.* All that time I seemed to sleepwalk through my life in Michigan, treating it as temporary, always waiting for the next trip to Cuba. I was in my early thirties when I began my treks from Michigan to Cuba and back. I was still young then, but I didn't know it. When I walked down the street in Havana, I no longer worried about being abducted. I was old enough to be confident. The men were also more subdued, and for good reason; this was the time of the "special period," when hunger was rampant. But men still whistled at me softly. One, I recall, begged me to go *hasta el fin del mundo*, to the end of the world with him.

Now it's different when I'm back in Cuba. Being in my fifties, I can no longer hope for such fervent male attention. I'm fit, I dance, I wear high heels, I color my hair, but I'm a middle-aged woman. I receive another form of praise, as if I were a well-preserved museum piece. A man, much older than I, impeccable in pressed slacks and a white shirt, passed by my side not long ago and said, "You look good, *señora*. You exercise, don't you? Diet, don't you? *Felicidades*, how well you conserve yourself."

They call me *señora*, not *señorita*.

That's how I know twenty years haven't passed in vain.

IT OCCURRED TO ME I COULD SPEND MORE time in Cuba and escape the dreariest months of winter in Michigan if I organized a semester abroad program. Like Persephone, I'd leave at the height of the cold and return in springtime, when the daffodils dot the landscape.

For the past two winters, I've traveled to Cuba with undergraduate students from the University of Michigan. I never expected this would be my fate: to be a teacher, a schoolmarm, in my native land. I teach a course in which we treat the island and its people as our classroom, visiting museums, artists' studios, ethnic neighborhoods, and architectural jewels in Havana and the provinces. We attend Santería religious ceremonies and we hike in the Sierra Maestra, where Fidel and Che planned the Revolution. In another course, I teach the students how to write creatively about what they're witnessing in Cuba. I spend many hours with them, much more time than I would back at Michigan, where I see students only in class and at weekly office hours. I tell myself it's worth it. Like a mantra, I utter under my breath, "You're in Cuba, you're in Cuba, isn't that wonderful?" And the days slip by.

During our three months on the island, the students stay in a penthouse dormitory with a stunning view of the Malecón and the glittering sea. The word "penthouse" summons up images of grandeur, but the building is in dire need of restoration and a coat of fresh paint, plus the elevator rarely works and the rooftop pool has been dry for years. Of course, the students enjoy the adventure of roughing it in Havana, gritty-urban-style. In truth, they don't rough it all that much. A warm and chatty grandmother and her hardworking granddaughter cook breakfast and dinner for them, mop and clean their rooms, and keep them company if they're lonely. The students also have access to the Internet from their apartment, a huge luxury in Cuba.

It's moving to watch my students immerse themselves in Cuban life. They take on Cuban gestures and start dropping consonants at the end of their words and find the courage to ride Cuban buses. Each and every student wants to have his or her unforgettable experience of Cuba: finding Cuban counterparts who play tennis or soccer or skateboard, or write poetry, or work in the theater, or do yoga, or study psychology, or sing opera, or rap, or brew beer, or engage in queer studies. They want to learn to coax music from the conga drums, not be stiff when they dance salsa. They want Cuban friends. They don't want to be tourists. Least of all do they want to seem like privileged *yuma*, the Cuban slang word for Americans. And inevitably I'm the one who must help the students fulfill their Cuban fantasies. They must be put in touch with like-minded people, coached, nurtured, and most of all, kept happy. *Unhappy on my island? That's impermissible.* Naturally I can't say that. I must be unfailingly sensitive to the needs of the students, be the perfect guide who leads each of them to find their own Cuba.

While there as a teacher in 2010, I ran into a colleague who was staying at a five-star hotel in Havana for a week while doing archival research. Smiling coyly, she asked, "Having fun babysitting the undergrads?" My face fell. *Babysitter*, she'd called me, letting me know I'm allowing myself to fall to the bottom rung of the academic ladder. "Yes," I replied, "I *am* having fun." Later I asked myself, Was I? And again I repeated the mantra that I *am* getting to spend more time in the country where I was born—and escaping the harsh winters.

Being middle-aged and a woman professor in Cuba can be sheer masochism. With my mortality looming over me, I'm made to feel even more acutely aware of my age as I traipse around Cuba with twenty-year-olds. My students are mostly women, and I find myself watching over them with concern, afraid they'll be harassed or that their hearts will be broken if they give their affection to a Cuban boyfriend who wants to use them to leave the country. I also can't help feeling a touch of jealousy toward these young women, these trusting Lolitas, whose curiosity and naïve smiles attract the attention and lust of Cuban men of every age and walk of life. When they receive catcalls, praise, and lingering looks, I want to protect them, spread a cloak around them and take them home, but then I recognize I'm being ignored, I'm invisible. Dare I admit I'm filled with sorrow when I see my students in the bloom of their youth wearing the white halter dresses I no longer can wear? Not to mention the short shorts I didn't even feel I could wear when I was young.

And yet, no matter how old I feel, I'll always be a little girl in Cuba. Having left as a child, I didn't make the decision to leave. I'm granted political innocence, welcomed with tenderness. "Taken out of Cuba," the locals say of me, shaking their heads. *"Ella no se fué. A ella la sacaron de Cuba."* On the island, I'm an eternal little girl. More and more, I feel like an old little girl, *una niña vieja*—a bit pathetic, concealing flabby arms under crocheted shawls, faithfully coming back, a witness to the unraveling of Cuba's hopes, wondering if it's too late, after all these years, to be part of the future of the island I can't bear to lose.

My father declared that if the ferry from Key West to Havana began operating again he'd go back. There's talk of that service beginning soon, but I doubt he'll follow through on his promise. My mother doesn't understand that I was the one who organized the semester abroad program with the Michigan students. She thinks the university has sent me to Cuba, stationed me there on a mission, something akin to military conscription. I don't try to correct this impression. I've learned from years of experience to be cunning and say little. What I know is that my travels to the island make my parents very anxious. They're still afraid for me. And I carry their fear like a bird trapped inside my heart, no matter how frequently I return. As a native, I'm obligated to travel on a Cuban passport. It doesn't matter that I'm an American citizen. As the moment comes to depart, yet again, for I'm forever reenacting our departure with every return, there's that last terrifying moment on Cuban soil. The immigration officer frowns while scouring my Cuban passport, always hesitating before letting me go. I worry: If I'm not allowed out, then what?

OLD LITTLE GIRL THAT I AM, I'VE OFTEN wished my parents could hold my hand as I totter in high heels along the broken streets of our Havana, where the roots of the banyan trees burst through the pavement and the cement disappears and yields to the red earth underneath. On that first trip with the students, just days after arriving, I tripped and fell flat on my face in Vedado, my old neighborhood, hurting my right arm so badly I couldn't pick up my pen to write. Nor could I dance because the simple twirl of my arm while being led in a turn caused me excruciating pain. My bruises lasted for the entire three months I was there.

I was so frazzled that prose felt too rational to get at the emotions that this experience unleashed. So I wrote a poem, "Broken Streets of My City." Here are a few lines:

> My city has broken streets.
> I have fallen.
> Been hurt.
> For months I sang
> an old lullaby to myself
> so I could fall asleep,
> the one my mother
> used to sing to me—
> *This pretty little girl*
> *born in the daytime*
> *she wants to be taken*
> *to the candy store.*

When I went back to Cuba again with the next group of students, I was careful to watch my every step, to walk slowly, deliberately, fearfully, as if the streets might swallow me whole.

IT USED TO BE THAT MY REENTRY PERMIT to go to Cuba would arrive only a few days before my departure date. I'd throw a few things into my suitcase and head down to the island. Going for a week or two, I could make do with little. Now that my trips are for three months, I find myself trying to carry my house on my back. Being older too, I'm not as willing to do without creature comforts.

Every trip to Cuba begins with a visit to the bank. Rent in Cuba, like most goods and services, must be paid for in cash. Bringing enough money for three months' rent, as well as for meals with students, tours, lectures, and unexpected emergencies, requires that I make a hefty withdrawal at my bank before leaving town. In Michigan, bank tellers are discreet; they don't bat an eye, don't ask where you're going with all that money. But I still feel like a crook walking out with a bundle of envelopes stuffed with hundred dollar bills.

Then the suitcases have to be packed with everything I expect to need and won't be able to find in Cuba.

I travel heavy—maybe I can blame that on leaving Cuba with my family in the early years of the Revolution. The Cubans leaving were punished for rejecting Communism by being forced to abandon their material possessions. To this day, the occupants of our old apartment in Havana still use the dining table, sofa, and bedroom vanity that belonged to my parents. Mami and Papi could take only one suitcase out of Cuba. Now I bring four large duffel bags, plus two bursting carry-on bags.

So what do I return to my country with?

Let me begin with the most embarrassing item. I confess I bring toilet paper, Charmin Ultra Soft. Toilet paper is in short supply in

Cuba. What can be found is rough on the skin. In most government buildings, you're lucky if you find sheets of the *Granma*, the national newspaper, wedged into the empty dispenser.

Baggies: I bring them small and large, with their handy Ziploc closures. They can't be found in Cuba at all. You don't realize how useful they are for the simple tasks of storing and sharing food until you don't have them.

I also bring Tupperware; it's expensive in Cuba, hard to find, and of poor quality. They're like Baggies—you only miss them if you can't get them.

I come prepared with fold-up sacks I keep in my purse. Stores in Cuba never have bags for purchases. Employees hoard them and sell them on the side.

I have a stockpile of fluffy towels, cotton sateen sheets, and two pillows. Guilt disclosure: I want to have the better quality of linens I'm accustomed to rather than the threadbare goods you get in Cuba. And there's a baby blue fleece blanket adorned with clouds. It gets cold in the winter in Cuba. It's a humid cold, making your bones feel as if they've been left to soak overnight in the ocean.

I travel with soap (Ivory), exfoliating body scrub (Origins), hand lotion (L'Occitane), shampoo and conditioner (Kiehl's), hydrating hair oil (Moroccan Oil), makeup foundation (Armani), eye shadow (Dior), eyeliner (Laura Mercier), mascara (Lancome), lipstick (Chanel), and lip gloss (MAC).

Basic medical supplies that I bring along include Band-aids, Tums, Advil, antihistamines, and a box of Kleenex to keep by my bedside, as well as packets of Kleenex to carry in my purse. Portable containers of hand sanitizer are essential. I bring several for use in public restrooms, where there is no soap.

Naturally I bring a laptop and blank notebooks to write in. I always hope I'll get a lot of writing done in Cuba, but words seem to fail me when I'm there. Life absorbs me, consumes me. From moment to moment, my feelings range from utter joy to the gloomiest melancholy. I'll scribble down some notes, but I don't write seriously until I'm sitting again at my oak desk in Michigan, where I conjure the memory of Cuba from a distance yet one more time.

As for clothes, I bring far too much black—stacks of black pants, black leggings, black skirts, black tops, black cardigans, and black dresses. Black is supposed to be slimming and elegant. That's why women professors wear it. In Cuba it's a color to be avoided. I get scolded for wearing too much black. Cubans say black retains heat and blocks the spiritual blessings of the *orishas* of the Santería religion. But I don't learn. I keep wearing black.

I come from a line of women who don't feel properly dressed unless we're wearing high heels. I fill up a suitcase with several relatively comfortable pairs, in a variety of styles, colors, and brands (Born, Aerosoles, Geox, Gentle Souls) to test them on the pavements of Havana and see if any can be worn without burdening the ever more sensitive bunions. Most recently (because I'm now so afraid to fall on the broken pavement) I've chosen to wear flip-flops (or rather FitFlops, with their thick cushiony soles) and carry the high heels in a tote, changing into them a block from my classroom to (hopefully) look tall and professorial as I saunter in. And I bring two pairs of salsa dance sneakers and a pair of tango shoes with purple stiletto heels. Tango dancing is catching on in Havana. There's a *milonga* twice a month sponsored by the Argentine Embassy, held in what was once a Jewish social hall on Calle Prado and which now is the Arab Cultural Center. I dance among ghosts, the Jews who've left and will never return to Cuba.

Not being an eBook reader, I brought an entire suitcase of books to Cuba when I went in 2010. I didn't have time to read all of them, but having the books next to my bed comforted me. When I told Cristy about the books, she looked bewildered. "Books? What you need to bring is a suitcase full of food." She told me about the Italian guys who rent her *casa particular*, how they bring pasta, tomato sauce, cheese, olive oil, basil, and pepperoni from Italy.

Cristy had a point: I thought about all the foods I missed while in Cuba and about the lack of fiber in the Cuban diet. Even with money, most of what can be bought in the stores is of inferior quality: lots of Spam, frozen chicken legs from the United States (since Americans eat only breasts), ancient canned goods, and yellowing mayonnaise. Beer, rum, and sugary sodas are never lacking. Only at the *agros*, the farmers' markets, can you find fresh fruit and vegetables, which are so ripe they must be eaten immediately before they rot.

So when I returned in 2011, I packed only a handful of books and filled up a suitcase with hefty purchases from Trader Joe's and Whole Foods: whole grain pancake mix, whole grain tortillas, rolled oats, ground flaxseed, brown rice, almonds, walnuts, pine nuts, peanut butter, olive oil, energy bars, and green tea.

I packed a whistling kettle, a nest of nonstick frying pans, and measuring cups.

I emptied my spice cabinet and tossed in curry, turmeric, ginger, parsley, cumin, bay leaves, and oregano, as well as a bottle of hot sauce.

I added multivitamins for good measure, along with chocolate calcium.

While we're on the subject of chocolate, I'll admit I couldn't resist bringing along, for my own selfish pleasure, to be eaten one square a day, three Barcelona Bars, my favorite of the exorbitantly expensive designer chocolates confectioned by Vosges.

I was a squirrel storing away my nuts for the winter—a winter in Cuba. I wanted to transport the first world to the third world, filling my suitcases with the trappings of my Ann Arbor bourgeois life. If my parents hadn't left Cuba, I'd never have had access to this life. And there I was, trying to carry it all with me. I felt ashamed being so greedy, but my need for material things outweighed my shame. And this made me more ashamed.

Such materialism was disdained in Tomás Gutierrez Alea's classic 1967 film, *Memories of Underdevelopment*, mocking the wife of the protagonist, who was departing for Miami after the Revolution. Rather than desiring such lofty things as justice, equality, liberty, she wanted Colgate toothpaste.

Too old for Colgate, I packed two tubes of ProNamel for my sensitive teeth.

I'VE WRITTEN ABOUT MY SEARCH FOR HOME in Cuba in an abstract, poetic way. But more and more, I long for a real physical home in Cuba: a piece of real estate.

"You want a home in Cuba? Divorce your husband and marry a Cuban."

That's one bit of advice I got.

The standard is one house or apartment per family, with two and three generations crammed into a small space. There are couples in Cuba who've gotten divorced in order to acquire more than one home. Afterward they remarry, but it's a complex legal process. Many lack the stamina or the cash to pay lawyers to carry out this transaction.

Foreigners can't possess a home in Cuba, though perhaps now that property rules are changing and Cubans are being allowed to buy and sell their homes, the day will soon come when they can. As a photographer I know put it, when I told him of my dream of a home in Cuba, *"Ponte en la cola"*—Get in line.

We stood talking on his charming Art Deco terrace, watching a group of boys tossing a ball in the Victor Hugo Park, surrounded by ficus and palm trees, the very park where I played as a child. He spoke with bitterness, telling me that his son from his first marriage had left Cuba for Miami because he'd given up hope of ever being able to have a home of his own on the island. He reminded me that his daughter from his second marriage, a talented art historian pushing thirty, still lived in the apartment with him and his wife, a curator of modern Cuban art. *"Ponte en la cola,"* he repeated, looking back at me sternly. "It's a long line. Thousands of people are ahead of you."

UP TO NOW, THE CLOSEST I'VE COME TO having a home of my own in Cuba is renting a *casa particular* and pretending it's mine. When I went with the students in 2011, I splurged and rented a two-bedroom, two-bathroom apartment around the corner from the former home of the writer Alejo Carpentier, who dreamed up the concept of "magical realism." This *casa particular* cost more than my mortgage in Michigan, but after two decades of renting a room in a shared apartment, which offered little privacy, and tolerating the previous year's dingy rental in a Soviet-era prefabricated building, I decided it was worth having a swanky place. I could be professorial, have the students over for conversation, and invite the guest lecturers from our academic program for lunch.

By Cuban law, landlords must reside in the homes they're renting to foreigners. I had the main floor to myself. The owners, a retired geophysicist, Gustavo, and his wife, Magalys, lived up a steep flight of stairs in a makeshift rooftop apartment with a miniature kitchen and bathroom. Furnishings included a formal dining table, and in the living room there were four antique rocking chairs with wicker panels, charming but in need of repair. Carved Buddha knickknacks brought back from a trip to China were lined up on the sideboard. The kitchen was large enough for yet another dining table. In Cuba, with the tropical heat, you can't have enough refrigerators. There were two—one worked better than the other—and in the pantry, there was a third refrigerator, which the owners used. In the master bedroom, I had a bed, a small desk and chair, two nightstands, a closet, and a dresser. Inside the drawers of the nightstands were packets of condoms. The shower curtain in my bathroom featured a monstrously enlarged image of a couple passionately kissing. But the condoms and curtain were wasted on me — I'd be living as chastely as a nun. The typical lodgers at *casas particulares* were male travelers, who preferred them to hotels, not to be hassled by security guards when they invited prostitutes to their rooms.

To come in and out of the apartment, Gustavo and Magalys had no choice but to walk through my kitchen, living room, and hallway to reach the main door. In the middle of the afternoon, I'd see Gustavo wander past, not saying a word, looking somber in his explorer's duck cloth hat. At the crack of dawn, I'd be startled by the sound of footsteps. I locked my bedroom door when I went to sleep.

I felt sorry for Gustavo and Magalys. Like my parents, they were in their mid-seventies. They deserved to enjoy life without having strangers occupying their rightful home. But they needed the money. There are very few subsidized goods available to Cubans — a roll of bread each day, some potatoes, a few split peas, a bit of rice. Soap, shampoo, clothes, shoes, and household goods have to be purchased in stores that had once been only for tourists. It's no longer possible to live in Cuba without money.

We shared a landline. Cell phones are mainly used as beepers in Cuba, since people don't have the money to maintain them. When the phone rang, both Magalys and I rushed to answer our upstairs and downstairs extensions. Rarely going out, Magalys sat around waiting for someone to call her. I had to answer by the second ring or she'd tell the caller I wasn't home. Sometimes I'd nearly kill myself rushing out of the shower to pick up the phone. If the call was for her, I had to say, *"Repita la llamada."* When the person phoned again, that was a signal to Magalys to pick up. Magalys never took phone messages; it was too much trouble to come down the stairs. But once, when my mother called, she scribbled a note: "Your mother called. Don't call her back."

Magalys's daughter-in-law, Celene, ran the business. She was clearly doing well. She had acquired an additional apartment, where she lived, in which she rented three rooms. A tight-lipped, no-nonsense landlady, Celene was married to Magalys's son, an engineer currently in Bolivia on an international mission sponsored by the Cuban government. Though she and her family were clearly "integrated" into the system, as people say in Cuba, her fifteen-year-old daughter was named Betsy (after Betsy Ross) because she'd been born on July 4. Celene breezed in at any time of the day, her dyed black hair flapping on her shoulders. She watched me with distrusting eyes. She liked to make a surprise appearance when I had guests over for lunch. I found this habit annoying and asked her several times to call me before coming over, but she never did. I noticed a surveillance camera installed at the entrance to the building. Celene claimed it didn't work, but she seemed to know when strangers visited. I wondered if Magalys reported from upstairs. In a rare moment of chattiness, Celene told me landlords in Cuba are supposed to keep a book with the names and addresses of those who visit the lodger, information they must turn in to the government. She'd refrained from asking for my guest list since I was associated with Casa de las Américas, a reputable institution.

Celene was so successful that she'd hired Cary as *personal doméstico* to clean and maintain the apartment. Cary, from a small town on the other end of the island from Havana, near the city of Santiago de Cuba, had a feisty wit. When Cary learned that I spoke Spanish fluently, she made me her confidante. Moments after we met, she told me she'd never had any luck in love and that she'd miscarried. She was hitting forty and feared she might never become a mother. She asked if I had any children. "One," I said. She smiled and said I was lucky. She offered to wash my clothes and to provide "gastronomical services" for an additional fee. With a countryperson's honesty, she told me that what I offered to pay was too generous and that she'd work for less money.

It was disappointing for Cary to learn I'd recently become a vegetarian. Not that I was the first vegetarian she'd ever cooked for; she'd had another one the previous year, also a professor from the United States. Whatever she cooked for me, she'd also eat, and she'd been looking forward to lobster, shrimp, and steak—the kinds of rich, savory foods that ordinary tourists desire when they're on vacation in Cuba and which most Cubans can't afford. But sadly, from her perspective, all I wanted were prosaic black beans and rice, alternating with lentils and red beans, salads made with cabbage, carrot, and tomato, the root vegetables of yucca and malanga, and fried plantains occasionally. Yes, she agreed, looking me up and down harshly, she'd make fried plantains for me only occasionally; they were too fattening for me to eat all the time.

Cary was eager to show me how well she cooked. She'd studied gastronomy and trained to be a chef. Her first day at the stove she was about to toss a Maggi bouillon cube into the beans. I stopped her and told her the bouillon cube contained monosodium glutamate and that this ingredient wasn't healthy. She looked perplexed, but listened. I'd seen Nestlé ice-cream bars for sale, even in the remotest corners of Cuba, and Nestlé was vigorously promoting their Maggi seasonings. Until recently spices had been hard to find in Cuba. All the eagerness for flavor had opened the door to MSG. Capitalism's dog was biting socialism's tail. But if I dampened Cary's enthusiasm when I vetoed her Maggi cube, it was only briefly. She was delighted I'd brought oregano, cumin, and bay leaves, as well as the Indian spices, and she used them with an exquisite sense of taste in all the meals she prepared for me, storing leftovers in the Baggies and Tupperware I'd brought.

Cleaning the apartment was also part of her job, but she despised it and glared at me if I walked into the kitchen after she'd mopped the floor. Washing clothes she liked even less. Early into my stay, she ruined a favorite cotton purple top by washing it with a cheap detergent that contained bleach. I was more distraught than I should have been. She dismissed this mishap by telling me the fabric was of poor quality. I ended up washing my delicates myself and gave her only my old jeans and white kurta tops. When I returned to Michigan, I sent the purple top back to Victoria's Secret, where I'd gotten it, and they sent me a new one. And I regretted having chided Cary.

One afternoon I arrived ten minutes late for an appointment I'd set up with a traveling manicurist and discovered that Cary was already getting her nails done. I was irritated because I thought I'd lost my turn and my own nails would remain ragged. "I'm almost finished," the manicurist said good-naturedly, completing a flower design on Cary's pinky. It turned out she'd come early, and that's why she'd had time to fit Cary into her schedule. A few minutes later, Cary's nails were ready. She elegantly got up from her seat and said, "Well, I can't work for an hour. I've got to wait for them to set." Where else but in Cuba, I thought, does a domestic worker get her nails done while on the job, and even beat her employer to it? Such equality, it seemed to me, was one of the positive outcomes of the Revolution, but Cubans, I also knew, are people who speak their minds and have resisted servility since the days of slavery.

Cary was also looking for a home of her own in Havana. As an outsider from Santiago, she rented a room in Cuban pesos (rather than in the expensive convertible currency I was forced to use as a foreigner) and hoped one day soon to acquire an apartment. She told me she had money saved up but hadn't found anything she could afford, except for a place that needed a new roof, and she wasn't sure it was worth the trouble. In the meantime, she was zealously protective of Celene's apartment (really Magalys's apartment) and behaved as if it were hers.

When I had a famous writer over for lunch, a winner of the national prize for literature, along with a famous composer, I opened up a bottle of white wine—there's now Spanish wine available for sale in

Cuba—and wanted to serve it to my guests. For weeks I'd admired the glass-windowed hutch in the living room that was filled with etched wine goblets. At last, I thought, I'd have a use for those fine goblets. As I went to open the hutch, Cary, as if detecting my actions by remote sensor, came running into the room. "Look, but don't touch," she said. Refusing to take no for an answer, I tried the hutch again, but it was locked and Cary wouldn't give me the key. "Here, use the regular drinking glasses," she said, and brought them out. "They're just the same."

I was upset that I couldn't treat my guests to wine in goblets, but Cary was responsible if anything in the apartment broke. Apologizing to my guests, I wondered aloud where I might buy goblets of my own. The composer said she knew of a woman who sold antiques out of her home and maybe she'd have goblets for sale. A few days later, I went, and sure enough the woman had hundreds of similar goblets, all stored in similar glass-windowed hutches. I imagined the people who'd drunk from them in the 1950s and left them behind when they fled the country after the Revolution. I retrieved several pretty ones in various shapes from dusty corners, ending up with twelve. After I bought them, I had no idea what I'd do with so many, but I still wanted them.

That night I washed the goblets until they sparkled and placed them face down on a white cloth atop a shelf in the kitchen. When Cary came the next morning, I pointed to them self-righteously and said, "I got my own because you wouldn't let me use the ones here." She smiled. "Don't worry, I won't touch your *copas* either."

I felt grotesque, flaunting my ability to obtain what Cary denied herself. I kept looking for occasions to use those goblets. Finally I thought I'd be able to offer wine in a goblet to the photographer who told me I'd have to wait in line for a home in Cuba, and to his wife, the curator, when they came to dinner. But they preferred Bucanero beer and Tu Kola soda straight from the cans.

DURING THOSE THREE WINTER MONTHS IN 2011, there were times when I marveled at how I went out at night alone, traveling from my rental apartment in Vedado to the oldest part of the city in one of the collective taxis fashioned from a 1950s American Chevy, an *almendrón* (literally, "almond husk"), as these iconic cars are known in Havana. I wasn't afraid as we meandered down Calle San Lázaro in the dark. Just before we reached the Parque Central, I'd say to the driver, *"Déjame aquí,"* Leave me here, and give him the fare of 10 Cuban pesos (50 cents) and close the door gently, having been scolded by other drivers when I'd slammed the door shut. Alone, in the night, and I wasn't afraid. I went wherever I needed to go. Afterward, at the corner of Neptuno, I caught another *almendrón* back to the apartment. "Are you going up Linea?" I asked, and the driver smiled and said, *"Sí, mi vida,* yes, my life, I am. Sit in the front, you'll be more comfortable." The *almendrón* filled with people and we plunged into the maze of broken streets, passing the great stairway at the entrance to the University of Havana, turning on Linea, the "line" where the streetcar once passed. Where had I gone that night? Dinner with visitors I barely knew who wanted to pick my brain about Cuba? Tango dancing in my stilettos? A rumba performance? I can't remember. But there was a night when I awakened to the shock of being utterly alone—as if I didn't have a husband, didn't have a son, didn't have a Mami and a Papi, as if I didn't have a house in Michigan, friends. Getting off at the corner of E Street, I walked the four blocks to the apartment and wondered if anyone was gazing at me from a window or a street corner, me in my black stretch pants, my black suede shoes, my ruffled black tunic, my handbag slung across my shoulder. I didn't rush. It was after midnight and the full moon lit my path. "You're a mature woman, a woman who has come into her freedom at last," I told myself, and slid the key in the door, walked into my bedroom, and locked myself inside. The next morning, after a heavy sleep, I opened my eyes and realized I'd dreamed that someone had seen me the night before and thought, "Look at that *extranjera*, that foreign woman. So alone, poor thing, so short of love, as if no one misses her."

FOR TOO MANY YEARS, DURING GABRIEL'S childhood, I'd say goodbye and leave him with David in Michigan and head off to Cuba. I don't know how I did it, since on every trip I fell apart inside. But there was a powerful magnetic force pulling me toward the place where I'd had only a short time to be a little girl before being taken away. Eventually I found ways to bring Gabriel along so I didn't have to be wistful in Cuba. On a couple of visits, we were able to go as a family, Gabriel, David, and I. It was Gabriel who played under the almond tree, Gabriel who experienced the thrill of jumping in and out of puddles during a tropical rainstorm, Gabriel who got to be a child, a teenager, and a young man in Cuba.

Now Gabriel is twenty-six. Both in 2010 and 2011, he came to spend the last ten days with me before I left Cuba with the students, willing to be there when I'm at my most discombobulated—not ready to leave but knowing I can't stay, frantic because the time has passed too slowly and too quickly, three months have come and gone and I haven't written, and I'm worried that Cuba has slipped through my fingers like water. And so during those last days, Gabriel and I are out and about in the broken streets of my Havana from morning until night, trying to keep the city from fleeing. We pound the pavement. I develop a blood blister on my left foot, but like a pilgrim who's made a vow to reach the shrine, I keep on going. Gabriel's an avid street photographer, and thanks to his pictures, I discover the Havana that surrounded me day after day but that I didn't know how to see. Having Gabriel with me, I relax into my role as mother. I'm no longer so agitated, no longer so sad about feeling old. I swell with pride as I introduce Gabriel to friends and watch as he greets women with kisses on the cheek, men with a strong handshake and bear hug, as one is supposed to do in Cuba. I hear him speak a languid island Spanish, which he rarely ever speaks back in the States, and I know I'm blessed to have this young man in my life, to have him as my son. Cuba may not be mine. A day may come when it will be his.

Gabriel feels as close to Caro as I do. Even when we're exhausted after a long day in the streets of Havana, he insists we go visit her. She's eighty-five, and her life has not grown any easier with the passage of time. One of her twin sons left for the United States and she hasn't seen him in eight years. Her other twin son is an alcoholic. Lately his drunkenness has taken a turn toward lacerating rage and self-destructiveness; his wife has left him, and even his twenty-six-year-old daughter can't bear to be around him. Caro's own daughter isn't of much help to her because she suffers from depression. It is Caro who attends to her daughter's two teenage children, making dinner for them every day. Though to my eyes Caro is beautiful, her long smooth hair brushed into two neat braids at the top of her head, she has lost all her teeth. But she doesn't dwell on her sorrows. When Gabriel asks if he can photograph her, she says he can take all the pictures he wants, then she shows him the photograph she keeps of him in her wallet—a school picture from the fourth grade I gave her once, when Gabriel's hair was blond and straight, before it grew as dark and curly as mine. "You're always with me," Caro says. I know Gabriel won't ever forget her love.

On our last couple of days, Gabriel and I often walk on Calle Obispo, an artery that runs between the Parque Central and the sea, where newly opened stores sell clothes, shoes, eyeglasses, home decorations, Che T-shirts, and old posters with messages like *Muerte al invasor* (Death to the Invaders) that appeal to tourists looking for authentic revolutionary souvenirs. One afternoon we stop to check out the pirated CDs being sold by a tall Afro-Cuban young man with pierced ears and a far-away look in his eyes. It turns out he is Gabriel's age. I ask him how his business is doing. Things are fine, he says, but he's sure he could be doing better somewhere else—if the chance arose to leave the country, he'd pick up and go in a heartbeat.

"And to which country would you like to go?" I ask.

Without batting an eye, he replies, *"Cualquiera."*

I repeat, "Any country?"

He nods. "Any country. I don't care which. Any country but Cuba."

How could this young man desire so badly to leave? I've spent years reflecting on diasporas and my need to return. But in Cuba there are people who desperately want to leave, to the point that they don't care where they land.

"Can we take your picture?" I ask.

"Go ahead," he says, and leans back against the wall of CDs.

Gabriel, who has been listening to this exchange, holds up his camera and quickly snaps a photo. He shows it to the young man, who thanks him. The young man's face comes out a bit blurry amid the display of CDs, but Gabriel doesn't try to take another photo. As we walk away, Gabriel says, "I only took one picture. I didn't want to be snapping photos if he doesn't want to be here."

THEN IT WAS TIME TO PACK UP. I was again the one leaving.

I'd rationed my precious imported food so carefully I had lots of leftover peanut butter, almonds, walnuts, pancake mix, brown rice. I made care packages for my friends and for Caro, to whom I also gave my oregano, cumin, and bay leaves (which are the primary things she always asks me to bring, year after year). And Cary got my hand lotion for her next manicure.

Three suitcases were staying behind, filled with belongings I wanted to keep in Cuba for my next visit. Cristy and Pepe, with their stoic kindness, had agreed to store more of my things in their already cramped apartment.

"Don't worry, Ruti, we won't open anything. It'll all be exactly as you left it when you come back," Cristy promises me.

Pepe does ask in which of the suitcases I've stored the Baggies. He's still using the three Baggies I gave him last year, washed and rewashed countless times. I tell him the Baggies are in the red suitcase, to take them all.

What will he think when he finds two unopened boxes of Baggies? Though Cristy says they won't peek inside the suitcases, I'm sure they will. How could they not? They'll find bed sheets and towels and toilet paper (I managed to save a few rolls) and frying pans and measuring cups and pillows. And the tea kettle. They'll find the antique goblets wrapped in layers of *Granma* newspaper.

I'll have many things waiting for me in Cuba, even beautiful goblets from the days of my parents' youth. So what if I don't have a home for any of these things? They'll be waiting across the hall from where I took my first steps.

That last night I can't fall sleep.

I think about all the nights I was alone, how I lived for the better part of three months in a strange solitude, just me and all the things I couldn't live without and had lugged to Cuba.

"You are an old little girl," I tell myself. *Una niña vieja.* And trying to be my own mother, I say, "It's late. Rest. Don't be afraid. Tomorrow's another day."

THE GREAT DIVA CELIA CRUZ, IN ONE of her last songs, an unusually sad song, "*Por si acaso no regreso*" (In Case I Don't Return), expressed her fear that she'd die without seeing her native land again. That reality came to pass: she did not return. I keep returning to Cuba for you, Celia, for you, Mami y Papi, for all those who don't return, can't return.

THIS IS AN ESSAY I CAN'T SEEM TO CONCLUDE. It's like a Cuban goodbye: you say goodbye, keep chatting, and say goodbye again, chat a little more, then offer yet another goodbye. So let me add a coda to the coda.

Back in 2010, after I tripped and fell in my old neighborhood, I was looking down at my feet as I walked, ever so carefully, not to fall again on the broken pavement. A man was approaching the same corner. I should have slowed down so we'd both have enough room on the sidewalk. But instead I sped up, charged forward, the way you do when the airplane lands and you jump into the aisle to claim your space. I got there first and brushed past. I glanced back, expecting him to be annoyed, but he smiled at me and said, *"Consérvese así, mi corazón."*

"Keep on being as you are, my heart." Those were his words, even though I'd been rude. *Mi corazón*, he said.

I climbed the stairs to my rental apartment and opened the windows. The sun was setting. The birds in the trees were chirping. It was the middle of March and the air was suddenly warmer. The winter had been quite cold in Havana. For several weeks, I'd worn a sweater to sleep and woken up pulling the blanket around my shoulders. On the coldest day, in late February, the sea flooded the low-lying streets near the Malecón—the wind and high tide sent the waves rolling over the walls of stone. The sea pushed its way to Linea and G Street. Water reached to people's thighs. Cars floated like rafts. Those streets once belonged to the sea, people told me, and the sea always comes back to claim what belongs to her. A few days later, once it was possible to be near the Malecón again, I stood next to three Afro-Cuban women who were singing to the female deity who resides in the sea, *"Agua, Yemayá, agua."*

So I was back in my apartment, sitting at the kitchen table that March after bumping into the sweet-tempered stranger on the street. I tried to write. Blackouts were no longer common, but a few sentences into the writing, the lights went out. Poof! Just like that, I was left in total darkness. Oh well. I readied myself for a quiet evening. Prayed my four eggs in the fridge wouldn't rot, eggs given to me by Cristy. It was a strange fluke, but eggs were available only through the rationing system during the three months I was there. They had run out of them in the hard currency stores; you couldn't buy them with money. If you wanted eggs, you had to get them from a Cuban who hadn't ever left the island, a Cuban with a *libreta*, a ration card.

I reached for the flashlight, shone it toward the ceiling. I wasn't scared, though I was living alone in a walk-up apartment on the top floor of a Soviet-era shoebox building constructed by a revolutionary brigade in the 1960s. If my mother knew, she'd have been scared for me. But she'd never know, I'd never tell her. In the dark, with just enough light to see my hand, I opened my laptop and began to write this story about being an old little girl in Cuba. I was using my left hand, since my right hand still hurt from the fall. I was typing letter by letter. I was discovering that my left hand was stronger than I'd realized.

An hour later, poof, just as suddenly, the lights came back on.

I should have kept writing, but I stopped. I put aside this story. I knew I wouldn't come back to it until I'd left Cuba. I save Cuba for when I'm gone. I need to miss Cuba, conjure Cuba, struggle to remember Cuba in order to write. All my writing comes from not being there.

Now I'm in my other home, in Michigan. This is where I'm sewing together the thoughts that were only loose threads in Cuba. I continually dive back into the immigrant experience of being a child who is taken out of her country, not knowing what's going on, not understanding that her departure is final, that she's losing her home. My eyes are in the back of my head.

Each and every time I worry: After so many returns, have I learned anything? Baba has been dead many years. Do I know the answer to her question now? Have I discovered finally what I lost in Cuba?

I have my ritual: I unpack my suitcases, look through scribbled notes, and torment myself with the question: So what did you bring back? Several months in Cuba . . . *y qué?*

Let's see. Well, to start, a stranger called me by the endearing words *mi corazón*.

And what else?

The ocean rose up and spilled over the walls of the Malecón and displayed her relentless force.

So?

I made pancakes with the eggs that Cristy gave me and they tasted divine, better than any pancakes I'd ever had, because the eggs were a gift: they couldn't be bought for any amount of money in any store.

That's all I have, fragments that I trip over, like the broken sidewalks of my Havana.

It's not much to go on, but I sit down at my oak desk and turn on the computer. I thank the spirits and my ancestors for my safe journey. Next I rub the beads on my evil eye bracelet to ask for good luck. And I start to write. I erase most of it. I write more. Erase. Write again. And erase. It goes on like this for a long time, until eventually some words remain on the page that I can live with. I know that if I hang in there long enough, I may be blessed. The pieces will form a story—and once a story is told it can never be lost.

Luggage ticket to Havana, from a
flight on Cubana de Aviación.

ACKNOWLEDGMENTS

First and foremost I must thank my parents, Rebeca and Alberto Behar, for their love and support. We began our journey a long time ago, when we left Cuba with my brother, Mori, and though there have been bumpy moments, I am grateful we survived and found courage and the path to mutual understanding and *cariño*.

I also want to thank the rest of my family, some of whom appear in this book. Hard as I try, I know my writing doesn't please them. I hope they will forgive me, again.

These stories have been written over a long stretch of time, from the beginning of our new century to just yesterday, and they have benefited from the careful readings of writer friends. My sincere thanks to the Latina Feminist Group, Tom Miller, Marjorie Agosin, Tish O'Dowd, Richard Blanco, and Erasmo Guerra, for all the ways in which they helped to make my writing stronger. Sandra Cisneros has been a constant source of inspiration through her writing and I thank her *de corazón* for her sisterhood and all that she does to support fellow writers through the Macondo Foundation. I am lucky to have the best writing buddy I could ever ask for, Ann Pearlman, a psychologist, novelist, and wise woman, who gives me free therapy while also pushing me to think about every word I'm committing to the page.

It has been a blessing to have Gisela Fosado as my editor at Duke University Press. We have worked together in many ways over the years, as teacher and student, as filmmakers, and now on this book, which she commented on thoughtfully every step of the way. I remain in awe of her calm, her strength, and her kindness. My debt to her is great.

I thank the entire staff at Duke University Press for their hard work on this book. Special gratitude goes to Judith Hoover, for her graceful copyediting, and Amy Ruth Buchanan for her lovely design and layout. It was an honor that Paul Stoller and Philip Graham were willing to read an earlier version of the manuscript and provide encouragement and astute critical comments.

Warmest thanks to Sandra Ramos for allowing me to use her stunning work of art entitled "*Y cuando todos se han ido, llega la soledad*" on the cover of the book.

Thank you to my dear friend, Rolando Estévez, for the beautiful drawing he allowed me to use inside the book, and for insisting that I never stop writing poetry.

The Department of Anthropology at the University of Michigan has been a wonderful intellectual space for me over the years, where I've had the freedom to pursue my own quirky vision of our discipline. I feel fortunate to have been supported in my goals by so many generous colleagues and thank them all.

The affection and faith of my teachers stay with me. Thank you to Mrs. Rodriguez, Hilly Geertz, and James W. Fernandez.

All the strangers who have treated me like family, I will never forget. Thank you to all those beloved people, in Spain, in Mexico, and in Cuba, who gave me a home as I tried to find where I belonged in the world.

David always waits for me to return from my travels and I love him for that and for his unwavering belief in me.

Gabriel keeps me honest and helps me to be a better person every day. I feel deeply grateful for all the journeys we have shared. And look forward to more.

—Ann Arbor, September 2012